John Stuart Blackie

Messis Vitae

Gleanings of Song from a happy Life

John Stuart Blackie

Messis Vitae
Gleanings of Song from a happy Life

ISBN/EAN: 9783337179991

Printed in Europe, USA, Canada, Australia, Japan

Cover: Foto ©Thomas Meinert / pixelio.de

More available books at **www.hansebooks.com**

MESSIS VITAE

GLEANINGS OF SONG

FROM

A HAPPY LIFE

BY

JOHN STUART BLACKIE

EMERITUS PROFESSOR OF GREEK IN THE UNIVERSITY OF EDINBURGH

χαίρετε πάντοτε.—St. Paul

London
MACMILLAN AND CO.
AND NEW YORK
1886

To the Students of
The Scottish Universities

PREFACE DEDICATORY

MY DEAR YOUNG FRIENDS — I dedicate this collection of lyrical fly-leaves to you, because there is not a little in it that owed its inspiration to the contagion of fresh young minds, and to the leisure for cultivating the Muse afforded me by the usage of what, in Scotland at least, I cannot but regard as the happiest of all human avocations, the profession of an Academical teacher. May you learn from these versicles what they are mainly meant to inspire, that reverential communion with Nature, the living poetry of God, that ready sympathy with all that is good in your fellow-beings, and that unswerving loyalty to the heroic traditions, the sacred shrines, and the heart-stirring melodies of our Scottish fatherland, which are of more value than much Latin and more Greek, and supply the purest atmosphere in which a happy existence and a fruitful activity here below may be achieved.

I am yours,

In the love of the good, the beautiful, and the true,

JOHN STUART BLACKIE.

UNIVERSITY,
EDINBURGH, *October* 1886.

CONTENTS

I.—POEMS AND SONGS

	PAGE
THE CHIEF END OF MAN	3
FAITH	7
ATHEISM	10
THE LAY OF THE LITTLE LADY	12
SPUT DUBH	17
MY WALK	22
MY BATH	26
ONWARD AND UPWARD	31
THE EMIGRANT LASSIE	34
MY SCOTCH LASSIE	37
THE CURSE OF SCOTLAND	40
RULES FOR A HAPPY LIFE	49
SONG OF A GOOD ECLECTIC	51
PESSIMISM	54
ITALIA	60
THERE IS NONE FREE BUT JOVE	64
CREEDS AND CANARIES	67

	PAGE
THE PRAYER OF SOCRATES	70
FEMALE BEAUTY	71
PORTRAIT OF A LADY	73
LOVE AND KNOWLEDGE	76
POLLY	78
THE THREE GRACES	82
AN APRIL SONG	84
'CUCKOO! CUCKOO!'	87
VACATION ODE	89
PASTEUR'S WORD TO YOUNG MEN	93
THE STUDENT'S FAREWELL TO SUMMER	96
A SONG OF GOOD COUNSEL	100
A SONG OF BACKGAMMON	103
A SONG FOR THE ROAD, AND A RULE FOR THE LIFE	106
BENEDICITE	110
HYMN	113
SONG OF OLD AGE	115

II.—SONNETS

RELIGION	123
THE TRINITY	125
CHRIST AND CHRISTENDOM	126
ATHEISTIC SCIENTISTS	127
CRITICISM	128
SUBJECTIVE AND OBJECTIVE	129

	PAGE
TO SCOTCH HERESY-HUNTERS	130
THE ORIGIN OF EVIL	131-132
Θέλω, Θέλω μανῆναι	133
WAR	134
OUTSIDE AND INSIDE	135
SICKNESS AND RECOVERY	136
ROBERT BURNS	138
CARLYLE	140
NORMAN MACLEOD	141
SYDNEY DOBELL	142
CHINESE GORDON	143-144
ALEXANDER PEDEN	145
THE BARONESS BURDETT-COUTTS	146
LORD ROSEBERY	147
DEAN RAMSAY	148
DR. WALTER SMITH	149
ROBERT LEE	150
LONDON	151
ENGLAND	152
THE SAVOY	153
THE DUKE OF ARGYLL	154
CLAPHAM	155
LALEHAM	156
TAYMOUTH CASTLE	157
THE DUCHESS OF SUTHERLAND	158
BONSKEID	159

	PAGE
LOCH BAA	160
ABSENTEE PROPRIETORS	161
BEN MUICDUIBHE	162
VENICE	163
LORD BYRON AND VENICE	164

III.—HISTORICAL BALLADS

ANCRUM MOOR	167
MERLIN AND KENTIGERN	175
PEDEN THE PROPHET	185
NOTES	198

I

POEMS AND SONGS

THE CHIEF END OF MAN

Natus est homo ad contemplandum atque imitandum mundum.
CHRYSIPPUS.

LOOK round about thee, and peruse
  With watchful-loving eye,
This vast high-hung cerulean dome
  Which mortals call the sky,
Studded with travelling lights; and this
  Green earth all gemmed with flowers,
Cinctured with seas, and leafy swell
  Of rich redundant bowers;
And with quick swarms of eager life
  All proudly peopled o'er,
Throbbing with rival hymns of joy
  From resonant shore to shore:
All this receive in truthful heart,
  And keep it mirrored there

As God's live record given to thee
  In picture-writing fair.
Nor stop thou here: but know that God
  This honour gave to man,
To image in his human range
  Some part of His great plan,
And work with Him as workmen work,
  And strive with faithful tool
To multiply the perfect type
  Learned in the Master's school.
Into the lines and hues of things
  With thought's fine feeling enter,
And what thy cunning brush charms forth
  To view makes thee a PAINTER.
Swim largely in broad seas of life,
  And what thou findest show it,
From deep-moved breast in rhythmic phrase,
  And men will call thee POET.
Or, if thou know soul-stirring sounds
  To blend with tuneful art,
MUSICIAN thou with wizard touch
  To tame each savage heart.
Or make thy poem of the stone
  To shelter and protect,

God of a marble world, and be
> A praiseful ARCHITECT.
Or know as ENGINEER to guide
> Blind forces with fine skill,
And bind the strong-breathed steam with bonds
> To work thy reasoned will.
Or with the mattock and the spade
> The sweatful honour claim,
To make the harsh clod teem with life ;
> Then FARMER is thy name.
And when wild passions toss their crests
> Beyond discretion's border,
The LAWYER thou to dam their swell,
> Within just bounds of order.
And when the prideful pranks of men
> Call forth the chastening rod,
Thou art a SOLDIER, and in thee
> The people own a God.
Or dost thou find the blood of men
> Sicklied with fever, then
Thou art the LEECH, and through thee comes
> God's healing touch to men.
Or, is the soul sick, then mount thou
> The PREACHER'S lofty station,

And from God's altar with pure fire
    Baptize the tainted nation.
Or wilt thou ride the sea with ships
    And the proud function claim,
To make all lands change gifts with all,
    Then MERCHANT is thy name.
And when class scowls on class, and scares
    Men's hearts with rude alarm,
The STATESMAN, thou, to speak the word
    That soothes the swelling storm.
Thus what we catch of God's high ways
    From the great cosmic plan
We image, as our skill may be,
    In the small world of man;
And, or by charm of Christian love,
    Or stern rule of the Stoic,
We make our little Earth sublime,
    Our little lives heroic.

FAITH

WHAT thing is faith? Ask thou the gleesome boy
    Who for the first time breasts the buoyant wave;
'Tis faith that leads him with adventurous joy
    To follow, where they plunge, his comrades brave.
Ask thou the boor who eats and drinks and sleeps,
    And loves and hates and hopes, and fears and prays,
Fishes and fowls, work-day and Sabbath keeps,
    And, where life's sign-post points his path, obeys.

Or ask the sage, with subtle-searching looks,
    Well trained all things in heaven and earth to scan;
Or ask the scholar primed with Greekish books:
    All live by faith of what is best in man.
Or him, sharp-eyed, with fine atomic science,
    The loves and hates of lively dust pursuing;
Who tortures Nature with all strange appliance
    To drag to light the secret of her doing.

Ask thou the captain who with guess sublime
    Mapped forth new worlds on his night-watching
        pillow,
And saw in vision a fresh start of time,
    Big with grand hopes beyond the Atlantic billow.
Ask thou the soldier who on bristling lances
    Rushes undaunted, breathing valorous breath,
And, where his leader cheers him on, advances
    To glorious victory o'er huge heaps of death.

Or ask the patriot who, when foes were strong,
    And faithless friends had sold their rights for pelf,
Waits till harsh need and shame rouse the base
        throng
    Into the high-souled echo of himself.
Ask thou the statesman, when the infuriate mob
    Brays senseless vetoes on his wisest plans;
Unmoved he stands, his bosom knows no throb;
    His eye the calm evolving future scans.

Or ask the martyr, who, when tyrants tear
    His quivering flesh, with calm assurance dies;
Sweet life he loves, but scorns to breathe an air
    Drugged with the taint of soul-destroying lies.

In such know faith, faith or in man or God,
    In thine own heart, or tried tradition's stream ;
'Tis one same sun that paints the flowery sod,
    And shoots from pole to pole the quickening beam.

God is the Power which shapes this pictured scene,
    Soul of all creatures, substance of all creeds ;
Faith intuition quick and instinct keen
    To know His voice and follow where He leads.

ATHEISM

(Written in a sleeping-berth of the yacht Santa Maria.)

THE sun shines on the waters; and the waters to the wall
Of my poor cabin, narrow, dark, and small,
Fling a perpetual unpurposed flow
Of luminous pulses dancing to and fro;
And from the wall the many-flickering show
      Shoots to my eye,
Far-travelled from its fountain in the sky.
Suppose me born and bred in such small home,
Cabined and cribbed, with never a look outside
      Into the heaving tide,
Or upward to the bright expansive dome
Which men call Heaven, what should I say of LIGHT?
I'd say, belike, it was a tangled maze
      Of freakish rays,
Flitting about to feed my wondering gaze,
Redeemed such-wise from Chaos and old Night,

A bright confusion without law or rule;
And for the SUN, the glorious lord of day,
And his all-permeant, all-plastic ray,
For that I knew no Sun, mayhap I'd say,
There is no sun in Heaven—and be a fool,
As atheists are—blind guides who go to school
With outward sense, and what mere sense compels
Alone believe. Be wiser thou, and know,
Behind all shadowy show
A causeful Substance dwells,
Behind all tangled maze
Of crowded things that try the wondering gaze,
In air, in water, and in teeming sod,
A Reason works, which wisely men call GOD.

THE LAY OF THE LITTLE LADY

A BALLAD OF MULL

In a tiny bay,
    Where ships lie sure and steady,
In a quiet way
    Lives a tiny lady;
In a tiny house
    Dwells my little fairy,
Gentle as a mouse,
    Blithe as a canary.

Travelling I have been
    In distant and in nigh lands,
And wonders many seen
    In Lowlands and in Highlands;
But never since the days
    When fairies were quite common,

Did human vision gaze
    On such a dear, small woman!

On the deep sea's brim,
    In beauty quite excelling,
White, and tight, and trim,
    Stands my lady's dwelling.
Stainless is the door,
    With shiny polish glowing;
A little plot before,
    With pinks and sweet peas growing.

And when in you go
    To my fairy's dwelling
You will find a show
    Of beauty, past all telling;
Wealth of pretty wares,
    Curtains, pictures, laces,
Sofas, tables, chairs,
    All in their proper places.

But above all fair,
    Of which my song is telling,
Sits my lady there,
    The mistress of the dwelling.

Dressed in serge light blue,
    With trimming white and snowy;
All so nice and new,
    With nothing false and showy.

Dainty is her head,
    Quite the classic oval,
Just the thing you read
    In the last new novel,
But you never saw;
    For Nature still is chary,
To reach the perfect law,
    She modelled in my fairy.

An eye whose glance doth roam
    O'er the azure spaces,
But still is most at home
    'Mid happy human faces.
Cheeks of healthy red
    With native freshness glowing,
By the strong breeze spread
    From purple moorland blowing.

And a look of warm
    Welcome to the stranger,

Whom the sudden storm
    Hath cast on her from danger;
And a board well spread,
    Bountiful and bonnie,
With milk and barley bread,
    Bramble jam and honey.

And for wit and brains,
    Though not taught at college,
Her dainty head contains
    All sorts of curious knowledge.
Every nook she knows,
    Every burn she crosses,
Where the rarest grows
    Of fungus, ferns, and mosses.

And when flowers are few,
    And suns of heat are chary,
She has work to do
    Beseems a bright-eyed fairy;
A telescope she keeps
    For lofty observation,
Through which she finely peeps
    At all the starry nation.

But she's more than wise,
    Better far than clever,
From whose heart arise
    Thoughts of kindness ever;
As the sun's bright ray
    Every flower is kissing,
All that comes her way
    Takes from her a blessing.

Where a widow weeps
    She with her is weeping;
Where a sorrow sleeps,
    She doth watch it sleeping;
Where the sky is bright,
    With one sole taint of sadness,
Let her heave in sight,
    And all is turned to gladness.

And now, if you should fear
    I'm painting out a story,
Ask, and you will hear
    The truth at Tobermory.
In beauty Mull excels
    All ocean-girdled islands,
And there this lady dwells,
    Sweet angel of the Highlands.

SPUT DUBH

(A Cascade near Pitlochrie.)

Son of the mountain,
Beautiful and strong,
Roaring and pouring
And sweeping along;
Mighty art thou,
As I see thee now
Flinging the gathered floods of the Ben
Into the leafy shade of the glen;
Like to a steed,
With galloping speed,
Tossing his mane,
And whisking his tail,
Art thou, when the pride
Of thy foaming tide
Leaps to the vale,
Son of the mountain!

Most like a god,
Of things that I know,
On the earth below,
Art thou, in the pride
Of thy foaming tide,
   Son of the mountain!
Summers and winters,
Inconstant ever,
Roll their changes
Over thy head;
Rocks tumble down
From the mountain's crown,
And stout old trees,
Root-wrenched by the breeze,
Fall with a crash
Into the dash
Of thy billowy bed;
But thou dost abide
Unchanged in the swell
Of thy sky-fed well,
Most like in thy pride
To a deathless god,
   Son of the mountain!

Wise was the old Greek man who sang,
"Water is best."
As from the breast
Of mighty Cybele,
Nurturing mother,
To every form
Of the breathing nation,
From eagle on wing
To creeping worm,
And man, the king
Of the vasty creation,
Flowed the redundant,
Life-sustaining,
Milky fountain ;
So, when thou pourest
Richly thy waters,
Budding and blowing
Follows thy flowing ;
Earth's sons and daughters
Rejoice in thy going.
Corn fields are waving
Near to thy laving,
Gardens are growing
With flower and with tree,

And proud cities rise
With towers to the skies,
Watered by thee,
   Son of the mountain!

Son of the mountain,
Lovely art thou,
Where thou leapest as now,
Silvery bright,
From the mountain's brow,
With the unspotted breadth of the blue above thee,
And the circling grace of the trees that love thee,
   Spiring larch, and the tresses fine
   Of waving birch,
And the red boled strength of the dark green pine,
Rejoicing with thee in the fair sunshine,
   Son of the mountain.
No fools were they who worshipped thee
So fair and bright, and wild and free,
   So beautiful, so strong.
They sought a god that they could see,
River god or nymph of fountain,
And poured their untaught litany

Responsive to thy bickering glee,
    Son of the mountain!

    Son of the mountain,
    Most like to a god
Art thou in the freedom and force of thy flow;
A God must be in thee, or near thee, I know;
    And Him I adore
    In this shrine of the glen,
    Mid the rush and the roar
    Where thy bright floods leap
    With silvery sweep,
Down from the crown of the old granite Ben,
    Strong son of the mountain!

MY WALK

*(Scene—*Ben Greig, Mull.*)*

YE gentle folks that live in town,
And on poor country wights look down,
And daily take your dainty ride
Mid courtly rank and Fashion's pride
In the Row, with dukes and earls
Lofty dames, and lovely girls,
God bless you all, and grant you pleasure
Up to the brim of your heart's measure!
But I have joys unknown to you,
And walks remote from London view;
    Where the burnie leaps with glee,
        And the ground is rough and hilly,
    That's the walk that's dear to me,
        Not Pall Mall or Piccadilly.

Where the torrent from the brae
Pours his strength and spreads his spray,

And, like a white-maned mountain horse,
Plunges down with headlong force,
Lashing the rocks with foamy sweep
Into the caldron dark and deep;
Where the birch-tree nods her plume
O'er tufted wealth of heather bloom,
And delicate ferns their wings uncurl
O'er the brown water's sleepless whirl,
 Beside a blasted holly-tree,
  With never a rose and never a lily,
 That's the walk that's dear to me,
  Not Pall Mall or Piccadilly.

Where from the great Ben's dewy crown
The infant rill comes trickling down,
And glances out beneath the crag
That cuts the sky with many a jag,
And creeps beneath the old gray stones,
Chips of the mountain's giant bones;
Then trips adown with easy pace
Over the huge slab's slippery face,
To rest a while in mossy well,
Where starry saxifrages dwell,
 With never a shrub and never a tree,
  Where the air is sharp and chilly,

That's the walk that's dear to me,
Not Pall Mall or Piccadilly.

Where the rough scour flouts the sky,
And the ragged wrack skirs by;
Where, round the granite's shattered peak,
Wild tempests rave and wild birds shriek;
Where, down the mountain's shelvy side,
Long streaks of pounded ruin slide;
Where thick the bare extent is sown
With blocks on blocks all rudely thrown,
And desolation, gaunt and grim,
Stalks o'er the huge Ben's leafless rim,
    I face the blast, erect and free,
        And, tho' you deem my fancy silly,
This mountain walk more pleases me
    Than your Pall Mall and Piccadilly.

Or where below, in peaceful glen,
'Neath the broad shoulders of the Ben,
The river winds in mazy error
From the bright loch's gleaming mirror,
Upon whose green and grassy rim,
With tower and turret quaintly trim,

Rises the house, beneath the wood,
Whose lord, true-hearted, kind, and good,
Preserves—a boast that few may claim—
His crofters better than his game;
  There, by the old and wide-armed tree,
   A theme for Paton or for Millais,
  I choose the walk most dear to me,
   Not at Pall Mall or Piccadilly.

Farewell! God grant you honest pleasure
Up to the brim of your heart's measure,
Amid the dust and din and stew
Of London town, which pleases you;
Amid the fair and flaunting show
Of prancing Fashion in the Row;
With gartered lords and ladies fine,
Who never without candles dine,
And tug of war in Church and State,
And clash of words in stout debate;
  From such high stir I would be free:
   In lone green glen or pasture hilly,
  A quiet ramble pleases me,
   Far from Pall Mall and Piccadilly!

MY BATH

(*Scene*—Kinnaird Burn, near Pitlochrie.)

COME here, good people great and small, that wander far abroad,
To drink of drumly German wells, and make a weary road
To Baden and to Wiesbaden, and how they all are named,
To Carlsbad and to Kissingen, for healing virtue famed ;
Come stay at home, and keep your feet from dusty travel free,
And I will show you what rare bath a good God gave to me ;
'Tis hid among the Highland hills beneath the purple brae,
With cooling freshness free to all, nor doctor's fee to pay.

No craft of mason made it here, nor carpenter, I wot;
Nor tinkering fool with hammering tool to shape the charmèd spot ;
But down the rocky-breasted glen the foamy torrent falls
Into the amber caldron deep, fenced round with granite walls.
Nor gilded beam, nor pictured dome, nor curtain, roofs it in,
But the blue sky rests, and white clouds float, above the bubbling linn,
Where God's own hand hath scooped it out in Nature's Titan hall,
And from her cloud-fed fountains drew its waters free to all.

Oh come and see my Highland bath, and prove its freshening flood,
And spare to taint your skin with swathes of drumly German mud :
Come plunge with me into the wave like liquid topaz fair,
And to the waters give your back that spout down bravely there,

Then float upon the swirling flood, and, like a glancing trout,
Plash about, and dash about, and make a lively rout,
And to the gracious Sun display the glory of your skin,
As you dash about and splash about in the foamy-bubbling linn.

Oh come and prove my bonnie bath; in sooth 'tis furnished well
With trees, and shrubs, and spreading ferns, all in the rocky dell,
And roses hanging from the cliff in grace of white and red,
And little tiny birches nodding lightly overhead,
And spiry larch with purple cones, and tips of virgin green,
And leafy shade of hazel copse with sunny glints between:
Oh might the Roman wight be here who praised Bandusia's well,
He'd find a bath to Nymphs more dear in my sweet Highland dell.

Some folks will pile proud palaces, and some will wander far
To scan the blinding of a sun, or the blinking of a star;
Some sweat through Afric's burning sands; and some will vex their soul
To find heaven knows what frosty prize beneath the Arctic pole.
God bless them all; and may they find what thing delights them well
In east or west, or north or south,—but I at home will dwell
Where fragrant ferns their fronds uncurl, and healthful breezes play,
And clear brown waters grandly swirl beneath the purple brae.

Oh come and prove my Highland bath, the burn, and all the glen,
Hard-toiling wights in dingy nooks, and scribes with inky pen,
Strange thoughtful men with curious quests that vex your fretful brains,
And scheming sons of trade who fear to count your slippery gains;

Come wander up the burn with me, and thread the
 winding glen,
And breathe the healthful power that flows down
 from the breezy Ben,
And plunge you in the deep brown pool ; and from
 beneath the spray
You'll come forth like a flower that blooms 'neath
 freshening showers in May!

ONWARD AND UPWARD

(*Motto of the Lorimers.*)

Onward and upward!
That be your motto, boys;
Bravely and blithely
Toiling through Earth's annoys;
Onward and upward,
Danger defying,
Sworn to be true men,
Living or dying!
    That be your motto, boys!

If there be any who
Fear the rude billow here,
Leave them to slumber
And rot on a pillow here!
We, with high-hearted

Daring, will enter here,
Like stout Columbus,
On seas of far venture here!
    That be our pleasure, boys!

Onward and upward!
Who would be sleeping here,
Let him lie low
With the worms that are creeping here!
But whoso has wings
Through thin air will be sailing here,
Not in the mud and mire,
Draggling and trailing here!
    That is our fashion, boys!

Whoso would live
Like a serf and a slave here,
Let him stoop to the lash,
Till he crook to his grave here!
But whoso would breathe
A free breath in the land here,
Let him stand in his place
With his sword in his hand here!
    That's what I do, boys!

What fired Martin Luther
With faith and with hope here,
To shake on his throne
The crazy old Pope here?
Just what made the Roman
To manage and master men,
Daring and doing
And scorning disaster then;
  That made the Roman, boys!

Onward and upward!
That's the true plan, boys,
To cast off the brute,
And to put on the man, boys!
If you don't rise,
The skies will not bend to you;
Downward and Devilward
Will be the end of you;
  Take that for a fact, boys!

THE EMIGRANT LASSIE

As I came wandering down Glen Spean,
    Where the braes are green and grassy,
With my light step I overtook
    A weary-footed lassie.

She had one bundle on her back,
    Another in her hand,
And she walked as one who was full loath
    To travel from the land.

Quoth I, 'My bonnie lass!'—for she
    Had hair of flowing gold,
And dark brown eyes, and dainty limbs,
    Right pleasant to behold—

'My bonnie lass, what aileth thee,
    On this bright summer day,
To travel sad and shoeless thus
    Upon the stony way?

'I'm fresh and strong, and stoutly shod,
   And thou art burdened so;
March lightly now, and let me bear
   The bundles as we go.'

'No, no!' she said, 'that may not be;
   What's mine is mine to bear;
Of good or ill, as God may will,
   I take my portioned share.'

'But you have two, and I have none;
   One burden give to me;
I'll take that bundle from thy back
   That heavier seems to be.'

'No, no!' she said; '*this*, if you will,
   That holds—no hand but mine
May bear its weight from dear Glen Spean
   'Cross the Atlantic brine!'

'Well, well! but tell me what may be
   Within that precious load,
Which thou dost bear with such fine care
   Along the dusty road?

'Belike it is some present rare
    From friend in parting hour ;
Perhaps, as prudent maidens wont,
    Thou tak'st with thee thy dower.'

She drooped her head, and with her hand
    She gave a mournful wave :
'Oh, do not jest, dear sir !—it is
    Turf from my mother's grave !'

I spoke no word : we sat and wept
    By the road-side together ;
No purer dew on that bright day
    Was dropt upon the heather.

MY SCOTCH LASSIE

If I had the brush of angel,
Dipt in colours rich and rare,
I would paint with choicest limning
My Scotch lassie fresh and fair.

Fresh is she as dewy morning,
Fair as blossom on the spray,
Fragrant as the birch tree waving
In the fresh breeze of the May.

O, my bright and blooming lassie!
Maids more stately well may be;
But no stateliest maiden ever
Breathed a smile so sweet as she.

O, my bonnie blithe-faced lassie,
Mild as bloom on hawthorn tree,
Rich as June, and ripe as Autumn,
Flower and fruit in one is she.

Saw you ever cowslip warmer
When the zephyrs came to woo?
Saw you bright-eyed speedwell peeping
'Neath the hedge with purer blue?

Warmer than her keen pulse keeping
Time to all things true and good,
Bluer than her blue eye swelling
In young love's divinest mood?

Softer floats no plumy sea-gull
Than her bosom's heaving charms,
Swan on lake not whiter swimmeth
Than the whiteness of her arms.

If I had the brush of angel,
Dipt in colours rich and rare—
No! no trick of brush or pigment
Ever limned a form so fair.

Let them limn who live in dreamland,
Where the brain-born phantoms sway;
I have feasted on the substance,
And the shadow pales away.

I will not make dainty mockery
With a painted thin display
Of a life that breathes and burgeons
With the fulness of the May.

I will see my dear Scotch lassie
In the ray that sweeps the hills,
In the bright far-shimmering ocean,
In the silver-flashing rills.

I will see her where the wandering
Bee sucks honey from the brae,
Where the mavis to the mavis
Pours his rich full-throated lay.

I will feed upon the sweetness
Of her presence near to me,
And her wealth of grace that hangeth
Like a peach upon a tree.

I will live on the dear memory
Of that hour of burning bliss,
When she lent her lips and thrilled me
With the rapture of her kiss!

THE CURSE OF SCOTLAND

'They that will be rich fall into temptation and a snare, and into many foolish and hurtful lusts, which drown men in destruction and perdition.'—ST. PAUL.

(*Written on occasion of the fraudulent Glasgow Bank failure in 1878.*)

'WOE unto thee, Scotland, Scotland! curse and commination dire,
Thou art blazing with a torch not lighted from celestial fire!
Once the angel Gabriel lent his sword into thine elect hand,
Now from west to east thou rangest with a sulphurous smoking brand;
Woe unto thee, Scotland, Scotland! thy soul's honour thou hast sold
For huge greed of glittering dust and gilded lies that look like gold!'

In mine ears this woe was sounded, whence it came I might not know,
Above me, in me, round about me, terrible, still it sounded so:
  Woe to Scotland, once true Scotland, once a star with stars in heaven,
Now a wandering death-blue candle, through destruction's limbo driven!'
Thus it sounded awful, awful, and I laid my head to rest,
And I prayed to God to smother the great terror in my breast;
But it sounded still within me, like a shriek and like a sigh,
Like the moaning of a tempest, like a murdered woman's cry.
Through my heavy sleep it sounded, as I tossed my fevered head,
Through my shrinking ears it echoed, like the gibber of the dead;
And a vision rose before me, through my sleep and through my pain,
And the gates of death were opened, and the dead men walked again,

And I saw a strange procession sailing slowly through
    the air,
Pale, but with a noble paleness, sad and solemn float-
    ing there,
And I heard the voice no longer, for a God was kind
    to me,
And he gave a sabbath moment from that cursing
    chorus free ;
And I looked, and, like Macbeth, a march of spectral
    forms I saw,
Mighty names, the pride of Scotland, blazoned with
    respect and awe,
Robed in sheets of Death's adornment, but with stars
    of glory crowned,
Shooting streams of kindly radiance through Night's
    pitchy bosom round ;
And the first I knew, COLUMBA, who from leafy oaks
    of Derry
Through the troublous whirl of waters steered his
    gospel-missioned wherry,
And with might of high volition, and with wisdom
    from above
Tamed the savage Celts and drew them with the
    gentle cords of love ;

And the second, tall and stately, with long locks of
    golden hair,
Was the WALLACE wight; a huge two-handed sword
    aloft he bare.
BRUCE, the third, the bravest King that ever hewed
    his thorny way
Sheer through danger to a throne; I knew him by
    the fair display
Of jewelled brooch upon his breast, and battle-axe
    whose weighty stroke
Felled the proud Bohun, and freed the land from
    England's galling yoke.
In the shadowy train the fourth, a noble youth of
    saintly mien,
A burning faggot in his hand, was gentle-hearted
    WISHART seen.
Fifth a mightier came than he, strong and stern, and
    in the van
Of churchly keen contention planted, fronting danger
    like a man,
Fearing not the threats of Princes, nor the sacerdotal
    ban,
Dazzled not by flickering smiles, nor melted by soft
    tears of beauty,

Listening only faithful-hearted to the high command
    of duty,
KNOX; with him the bold Protester, lion-hearted
    RENWICK came,
In his hand a cross and tower with 'Sanquhar' writ
    in words of flame;
Who came next I knew from eye hot-flashing with
    intensest fire,
On his lip the scorn of baseness, in his hand a sound-
    ing lyre,
BURNS, the ploughman-bard; behind him one of
    mellower blood than he,
Healthy-hearted, and with large rich swell of various
    minstrelsy;
From his eye there streamed a sweetness like the sun
    in flowery May,
On his Jovian forehead thoughts of kingly range did
    mildly sway,
SCOTT; and in his hand he held the rose and thistle
    twined together,
And on his breast, and near his heart, a blooming
    tuft of purple heather.
Then I saw three mighty prophets closing in the long
    array,

Prophets whom mine eyes had worshipped when they
   dwelt in house of clay.
CHALMERS first, with fervid chariot, flashing fire from
   flinty stones,
Breathing blasts of quickening virtue o'er the valley
   of dry bones;
GUTHRIE next, festooned with flowers, and picking
   glory from the ground,
Flinging with redundant mirth rich sheaves of mellow
   jest around.
Then MACLEOD, with large strong heart, from bonds
   of base convention free,
Wise from life's o'erflowing wells to mingle godliness
   with glee.
These I saw, a pomp of ghosts in procession pale and
   slow,
And I looked and feared and listened; and again the
   sound of woe
Pierced my ears; and that dire chorus cursed again,
   and sounded so:
' *Woe to Scotland, woe and wailing, once the honest and
   the true,*
*Cousined now with rogues and sharpers, subtle Greek
   and swindling Jew!*'

And I looked and saw and lo! on the ground a virgin lay
With a healthy hue, well favoured, clad in weeds of sober gray,
But on her brow an ugly gash, and dimness floating in her eye,
And her broad full bosom heaving with the frequent sob and sigh;
In her right hand she held a tuft of heather from whose purple store
Gushed—O God! a bloody spout, and with red murder drowned the floor;
From her left a thistle rose, and every prickle where it grew
Turned to steel, and stabbed her flesh, and striped her vest with crimson hue;
And at her foot a book there lay, soiled and rent in many a rag,
A holy book, and near the book a fat, well-nurtured money-bag,
Dyed with blood; and o'er her head a grinning big-mouthed demon stood,
And dogs with him, a red-haired brood, that ever licked the streaming blood.

O God! O God!—I would have waked; but heavy bonds held down my breast;
I stopped my ears; but still I heard the woeful cry that would not rest,
As each shape in that procession, with sepulchral moan sonorous,
Pointing to the bleeding maiden sharply toned the cursing chorus—
'Woe to Scotland, woe and wailing, curse and commination dire,
Thou art fallen, fallen, fallen low with Sidon and with Tyre!
Damned lust of gold hath bound thee, O our country, damn'd indeed,
Thy most sacred birthright bartered basely for insatiate greed;
All thy proud distinctions razed, and on thy brow that brightly shone,
Sullen clouds and ugly scars, red-handed murder calls her own;
And all the air is rent with cries, and all the sky is raining tears,
And widows weep, and orphans wail, and old men curse their length of years,

And all thy hymns are turned to curses, curse and
    commination dire ;
The woe of Babylon is thine ! the curse of Sidon and
    of Tyre ; '
And the recording angel writes—' Woe to Scotland !
    thou hast sold
Thy soul's loyalty for dust, and glittering lies that
    look like gold ! '
I heard; I saw; mine eyes were coal ; mine ears were
    hissing furnace ; I
Writhed in my rest, and burst the bonds of painful
    sleeping with a cry ;
I rose and dressed, and walked abroad, and lo ! my
    dreaming was no dream,
I found the curse in every street, in every talker's
    common theme.

RULES FOR A HAPPY LIFE

Wouldst thou be a happy liver,
Happy, and studious to enhance
The glory of the great Life-Giver,
Launch not thy boat to drift at chance
Where strong floods roll and wild waves dance
    On life's broad-rushing river.
Live as a man, and count it treason
To man to live divorced from reason;
Prove your ground, and know your game,
And ply your task with stout endeavour,
Nor courting praise, nor fearing blame.
Know your own worth, and know not less
Your neighbour's weight and worthiness;
And, where he works well, let him do
The work that might be spoiled by you.
Make a good friend where'er you can;
Not wise is he who hath no eyes
To know how fools may help the wise;

With loving deeds bind man to man,
But never shrink with blinking eye
From what they only learn who try ;
And, though you stand alone, in sight
Of God be bold to hold the right.
March bravely on, and, if you stumble,
Never groan and never grumble ;
Rise again with wise forgetting ;
Wounds were never salved by fretting.
Watch your chance, and know your hour,
And let the moment feel your power ;
Shape your path, and keep your rules
With deaf ear turned to meddling fools.
'Tis dull to wait, and hard to stand,
But God's time comes with high command,
That claims the service of your hand.
Let the wise farmer teach you knowledge,
Oft sought in vain at school and college ;
Split the rock, and turn the sod,
With busy hand cast honest seed,
Stoutly uproot each harmful weed,
And let the seasons wait on God !

SONG OF A GOOD ECLECTIC

German Air—'Seit Vater Noah im Becher goss.'

My creed and my master you wish to learn?
   I really can't answer you so,
It never gave me grave heart-concern
   My name or my title to know;
     I love all the good and the fair;
       And when prophets come near me,
       To warn or to cheer me,
         I take off my hat
        To this one and that,
     But to none in all points I can swear.

You know what the great Apostle Paul
   In his wise Epistle says,
The body is one, and the members all,
   Have rights in their several ways;
     And to this I am willing to swear

With head clearly knowing,
And heart warmly glowing,
And firm hand to strive,
Completely alive,
All good things to do and to dare.

My head I have given, now understand,
To Aristotle the wise,
All things to know sublime and grand,
And scan with critical eyes;
And like him no labour I spare,
With fine speculation
And large tabulation
To blazon the glory
Of life's wondrous story
In the land, and the sea, and the air.

My heart I give, my noblest part,
To Christ the Lord who gave
Our faith new scope with the glorious hope
Of life beyond the grave;
And no honest labour I spare,
To stamp on each real
The godlike ideal,

And with triple-mailed breast
To fight for the best,
And the load with the laden to share.

My stout right arm to Zeno I give,
  Well poised for a weighty blow,
With friends a faithful friend to live,
  To foes a fearful foe.
    Thus the badge of the Stoic I wear,
      Not fretful and tearful
      But constant and cheerful,
        To do on a plan
        The service of man,
    And stoutly to bear, and forbear.

Then Epicurus, good easy man,
  I really don't wish to exclude ;
I give him my left—'tis all I can—
  For pleasure is cousin to good ;
    And surely to banish dull care
      With a glass brightly brimming,
      And an eye softly swimming,
        And a snatch of a song
        Can never be wrong,
    When wise moderation is there !

PESSIMISM

BRIGHT-FACED maiden, bright-souled maiden,
    What is this that I must hear?
Is thy heart with sorrow laden,
    Is thine eye dimmed with a tear?
Can it be that lips so sweetly
    Rounded to be kindly kissed,
Could be twisted indiscreetly
    To that vile word *Pessimist?*
Not for thine own ills thou weepest;
    Softly feathered is thy nest;
When thou wakest, when thou sleepest,
    Thou art fortuned with the best.
But thy sisters and thy brothers
    Pierced with many a woeful smart,
Dying children, wailing mothers,
    Fret thy nerve, and stab thy heart.

In the country, in the city,
 Godless deeds, a loveless list
Stir thy blood and move thy pity,
 And thou art a PESSIMIST.
Storms and wars and tribulations,
 Fevered passions' reinless tide,
With insane hallucinations
 Mingled, travel far and wide.
Can there be an Eye inspecting
 Things so tumbling in pell-mell,
With a cool control directing
 Such a hotbed, such a hell?
Nay, sweet maid, but think more slowly;
 Though this thing and that be sad,
'Tis a logic most unholy
 That the gross of things is bad;
'Tis a trick of melancholy,
 Tainting life with death's alloy;
Or in wisdom, or in folly,
 Nature still delights in joy.
Dost thou hear of starving sinners
 Nine and ten or ninety-nine?
Many thousands eat good dinners,
 Many hundreds quaff good wine.

Hast thou seen a score of cripples?
    Equal legs are not uncommon;
If you know one fool that tipples,
    Thousands drink not—man and woman;
Tell me, if you know, how many
    Murders happen in the town?
One a-year, perhaps, if any;
    Should that weigh your heart quite down?
No doubt, if you read the papers,
    You will find a strange hotch-potch,—
Doting dreams, delirious capers,
    Many a blunder, blot, and blotch;
Bags of windy speculation,
    Babblement of small and great,
Cheating, swindling, peculation,
    Squabblement of Church and State;
Miners blown up, humbugs shown up,
    Beaten wives, insulted brides,
Raving preachers, witless teachers,
    Lunatics and suicides;
Drains and cesspools, faintings, fevers,
    Poisoned cats and stolen collies,
Simple women, gay deceivers,
    Every sort and size of follies,

Wandering M.P.'s brainless babble,
    Deputations, meetings, dinners,
Riots of the lawless rabble,
    Purple sins of West-End sinners;
Driving, dicing, drinking, dancing,
    Spirit-rapping, ghostly stuff,
Bubble schemes, and deft financing,
    When the shares are blown enough.
All this is true; when men cut capers
    That make the people talk or stare,
To-morrow, when you ope the papers,
    You're sure to find your antics there.
But you and I and all our neighbours,
    Meanwhile in pure and peaceful ways,
With link on link of fruitful labours,
    Draw out our chain of happy days.
See things as they are; be sober;
    Balance well life's loss and gain:
If to-day be chill October,
    Summer suns will come again.
Are bleak winds for ever sighing?
    Do dark clouds for ever lower?
Are your friends all dead and dying?
    All your sweetness turned to sour?

Great men no doubt have sometimes small ways,
    But a horse is not an ass,
And a black snake is not always
    Lurking in the soft green grass.
Don't be hasty, gentle lady;
    In this whirl of diverse things
Keep your footing, and with steady
    Poise control your equal wings.
All things can't to all be pleasant,
    I love bitter, you love sweet;
Some faint when a cat is present,
    Rats find babies' cheeks a treat.
If all tiny things were tall things,
    If all petty things were grand,
Where will greatness be, when all things
    On one common level stand?
Do you think the wingèd breezes
    Fraught with healthy ventilation,
When a tender infant sneezes
    Should retreat with trepidation?
When dry Earth to Heaven is calling
    For soft rain and freshening dew,
Shall the rain refrain from falling
    Lest my lady wet her shoe?

Fools still rush to rash conclusions,
    And the mole-eyed minion man
Talks of troubles and confusions,
    When he sees not half the plan.
Spare to blame and fear to cavil,
    With short leave dismiss your pain,
Let no fretful fancies revel
    In the sanctum of your brain.
Use no magnifying glasses
    To change molehills into mountains,
Nor on every ill that passes
    Pour hot tears from bitter fountains.
Trust in God and know your duty,
    Some good things are in your power;
Every day will bring its booty
    From the labour of the hour.
Never reck what fools are prating,
    Work and wait, let sorrow lie;
Live and love; have done with hating,
    Goethe says—and so say I.

ITALIA

(Written on the rail on the road between Florence and Pisa.)

I

ITALIA! how I love thee, with thy brightness and thy
    beauty,
And thy flush of vivid verdure in the shining month
    of May!
    With thy vines all richly swinging,
    And thy blithe birds sweetly singing,
    And thy bells of worship ringing,
        In the shining month of May;
    With thy stout old castled places
    With severe, majestic faces,
    Hung round with storied graces,
        In the brightness of the May;
    With thy towers that look serenely
    From their proud cliffs, throned so queenly,
    With broad mantle flaunting greenly
        In the brightness of the May;

With thy streams so grandly sweeping,
And thy airs so softly sleeping,
And thy fountains freshly leaping
  In the bright face of the day ;
With thy names that fill the ages,
Statesmen, singers, saints and sages,
And thy shrines with pictured pages
  In significant display ;
With mighty memories near thee
In strength to atmosphere thee,
From dismal doubt to clear thee
  When falls the cloudy day :
With thy years of long probation
For the glorious consummation
To wear the name of NATION
  In the brightness of to-day :
Italia, I will love thee in thy grandeur and thy glory,
And thy wealth of spreading beauty in the shining
  month of May !

II

But, Italia, I may never change the land that I was
  born in

For thy beauty and thy splendour and thy triumph
    in the May,
  The land of lofty Ben,
  And of green, far-winding glen,
  And of light-heeled, kilted men,
    On the purple heather brae ;
With crystal wells clear gushing,
And amber torrents rushing,
And bright September flushing
    With the heather on the brae :
With the wide Atlantic's roar
On the gray and granite shore,
And the pure dew's dripping store
    On the greenness of the brae ;
Where the fragrant birch-tree waves
O'er the hollow mountain caves,
And the headlong-tumbling waves
    Dash the glory of the spray ;
The land where first I drew
Sweet breath of life, and grew
Hard of foot, and fresh of hue
    As the heather on the brae ;
The land that never quailed
When the haughty foe assailed,

And whose mettle never failed
  In the patriotic fray,
And whose sons aye stand together
For the thistle and the heather,
In the bluster of the weather,
  Or the mildness of the May;
Brave land where I am rooted like the pine-tree on the mountain,
I have loved, and I will love thee, while the sun shall rule the May!

THERE IS NONE FREE BUT JOVE

Οὐδεὶς ἐλεύθερος, πλὴν Διός.—ÆSCHYLUS.

'THERE is none free but Jove;' thus speaks
    A weighty old tragedian,
Who sang whilom to tuneful Greeks
    In Doric airs and Lydian;
And wisely sang—for truth and right,
    Once true, are true for ever,
Even as the sun pours forth his light
    With strength that faileth never.

Who's free?—a king?—Who first must please
    Before he rule a people,
And turn him lightly to the breeze,
    Like cock upon the steeple!
A priest—a churchman?—who to fan
    The people's hot devotion,
Must fear to stretch his faith a span,
    Beyond their narrow notion.

Who's free?—a democrat?—no more
    Than any salt sea bubble,
When far-drawn billows rage and roar,
    Is free from yeasty trouble;
No more than Autumn leaves are free
    To choose their place of falling,
When sea-birds shriek from sea to sea,
    And blast to blast is calling.

Who's free?—the lawyer?—not he, bound
    With knots of old traditions,
His reason prisoned round and round
    With clauses and conditions;
Whose thought to mouldy record clings,
    Who loves to walk in fetters,
And chokes the sacred soul of things
    With rolls of old black letters.

Who's free?—the scholar?—no; not he
    The slave of printed paper,
Who where the sun is free to see,
    Lights his own twinkling taper,
And from much nonsense picks some sense
    And makes a mighty clamour,

And strangles living eloquence
    In mummy bands of grammar.

Who's free ?—the statesman ?—ask the man
    Who fain would do a little,
But shrinks back from the factious clan
    That snaps at every tittle,
And fears his party most of all,
    Who, at his boldness frowning,
May cast him with a weighty fall
    From out the street called Downing!

There is none free but Him above,
    The mighty Lord of all things,
With bond of everlasting love
    Who binds both great and small things.
And who treads Earth with pure intent
    To search into His wonders,
Will live least slaved to sinful bent,
    Most free from evil blunders.

CREEDS AND CANARIES

I HAD a sweet canary bird,
Whose little wing was never stirred
    Beyond the wires around it;
I looked upon my dainty bird,
And, while I looked, my heart was stirred
To think that pretty prisoned thing
May never flap its native wing
    Beyond the bars that bound it!

I went and ope'd the little door,
And looked; but, sooth, I wondered sore
    To see my small canary:
With jerking head and pecking bill,
Within the wires it tarried still,
And had no lust abroad to spring,
And flit about with ransomed wing
    In ample range and airy!

Well, well! quoth I, 'tis plain to see
You have no notion to be free,
    So stay within your cage now!
And yet, methinks you are no fool,
And, safely bound by customed rule,
You wisely shun a larger home,
Where cats and deathful dogs may roam,
    If you should leave your cage now!

If birds are wise, men are not fools,
For they too have their customed rules
    And pretty gilded cages;
And, should you wish to make them free,
Just ope the door, and you will see
No folded wing they 'gin to stir,
But much the prudent ease prefer
    Of their own gilded cages.

The lawyer and the grave D.D.,
Who find strong bond of unity
    In old time-hallowed pages,
With sanctioned text and hoary creed
And fond tradition serve their need,
And live as safe and shielded well

As lobsters in close-mailèd shell,
   Or birds in gilded cages.

And, though you make a dusty din,
They wrap them closer in their skin,
   And con their ancient lessons ;
And they are wise ; for who can tell
What risks may lurk and dangers fell
To helmless souls all tossed about
In seas of drivel and of doubt,
   Unmoored from old Confessions ?

THE PRAYER OF SOCRATES

Καὶ εὔχετο δὲ πρὸς τοὺς θεοὺς ἁπλῶς τἀγαθὰ διδόναι
ὡς τοὺς θεοὺς κάλλιστα ἐιδότας ὁποῖα ἀγαθά ἐστι.
                                XENOPHON, *Mem.* 1, 3, 2.

GRANT, O Olympian Jove supreme,
Not my wish, and not my dream;
Grant me neither gold that shines,
Nor ruddy copper in the mines,
Nor power to wield the tyrant's rod,
And be a fool, and seem a god,
Nor precious robe with jewelled fringe
Splendid with sea-born purple tinge,
Nor silken vest on downy pillow,
Nor hammock hard on heaving billow;
But give all goodly things that be
Good for the whole and best for me.
My thoughts are foolish, blind, and crude;
Thou only knowest what is good.

FEMALE BEAUTY

A LOVELY woman?—well, a flower
In blushing bed, or shady dell,
With spreading crown, or drooping bell,
That glories in its growing power,
The triumph of the sunny hour,
Is beautiful; even so the trees
That fling their tresses to the breeze,
All fragrant with the breath of spring,
What time the leafy copses ring
With song of birds. But to be fair
Only as flowers and trees are fair,
With shapely form and colours rare,
And perfume sweetening all the air,
Is to be less than woman. Not
Pure-tinctured skin without a blot,
Nor merry blood that lightly flows
Rejoicing as it comes and goes,

Nor stature tall, nor brow serene,
With port and posture of a queen,
Nor full blue eyes that overbrim
With swelling life, nor rounded limb,
Nor ivory neck, nor lily arms,
Nor chiselled mouth with subtle charms,
Nor dimpled cheek, nor rosebud lips,
Nor dainty foot that lightly trips
And scarcely stirs the heather tips,
Nor fingers fine from tuneful board
That charm the sweetly blended chord;
Not these: all these fair maid may show,
A faultless mould from top to toe,
Yet lack the one thing that makes woman
More than the daisy on the common,
The one fair thing to mortals given
To bridge the gap from Earth to Heaven:
  The inspiring soul that to a godlike grace
Attunes each move, and spreads a glory o'er the face.

PORTRAIT OF A LADY

PAINT me your perfect lady. I have seen
Some part, perhaps the whole, of what I mean;
Yet in articulate feature to declare
The form that haunts my thoughts divinely fair
May well outrange my skill; but thy request
Strikes all denial dumb. No broad display
Of rustling flounces marks her gentle way,
But like the breezes of the light-winged May,
Softly she comes, and fragrant all as they.
Oh, she is lovely! all the summer dwells
In her bright eyes, and every feature tells
A treasured sweetness in the soul within,
That beats like music through the lucid skin;
And, when she speaks, soft silvery accents flow
Full-throated from a mellow depth below,
Not clipt in shreds, nor with a tinkling din,
A shallow plash from hollow heart within.

Not bold is she to place herself before
The first, nor slinks demure behind the door,
But takes her place just where she ought to be,
Nor makes you feel, when there, that it is she.
With native grace, and fine untutored mien,
She greets the poor, or stands before a queen,
Sweeps with light floating ease the festal floor,
Or bends o'er sick beds with the suffering poor.
She hath no postures, knows no attitudes;
Her unschooled gesture gently shows her moods;
She casts no proud and patronising eye
On those below, nor cringes to the high.
All things to all she is: for why?—in all
Her skill is to be true and natural,
True to herself, and to the high ideal
That God's grace gave to her to inform the real;
True to her kind, and to your every feeling
Respondent with a power of kindliest healing.
She knows no falseness; even the courtliest lie
She dreams not; truth flows from her deep blue eye;
And, if her tongue speaks pleasant things to all,
'Tis that she loveth well both great and small;
And all in her that mortals call politeness,
Is but the image of her bright soul's brightness

Direct from heaven.   Such is the perfect fair
Whom in my heart I hold, and worship there;
And, if the picture likes thee well to see,
Know, lady, more than half I stole from thee!

LOVE AND KNOWLEDGE

Give me a smile of lovely woman,
    The glowing cheek, the loving eye,
And I'll count all things cheap and common
    That books can teach, or gold can buy.
Add field to field, nor stint your measure,
    Heap bales on bales to swell your store,
One little kiss outweighs your treasure
    From lips with sweetness streaming o'er.

Some men there be, a curious nation,
    Who strive all knowable to know,
And register with nice summation
    Things dry as dust, and cold as snow;
But give to me the flower that bloweth
    With fragrance from the balmy south,
The quickening power of love that floweth
    From eye to eye, from mouth to mouth.

What profits me the shell to gather
  Of snake or lizard, newt or toad,
That crawled on earth ere our prime father
  Looked wondering on his green abode?
Let the dead to the dead be giving
  What dusty good they have to give;
Life is my school, and with the living,
  While I have strength to live, I live.

Go take thy glass and scan the planet,
  Besmoke the moth, and cut the worm,
And, though thy wit be weak to ban it,
  Take nice account of coming storm;
But give, O give me, sweet-souled woman,
  Thy gracious smile, thy loving eye,
And all things else I'll count quite common
  That books can teach, or gold can buy!

POLLY

WHO will show us any good?
    Said a fool once in his folly;
If he knows what thing is good,
    Let him come and see my Polly!
Who is Polly? Blithe and gay
    Polly is the parson's daughter;
You may see her any day
    On the banks of Cluny water.

Who shall show us any good?
    Said a fool once in his folly,
In a sullen, sceptic mood,
    Sulky and self-centred wholly.
If he has an eye to see
    Sights that banish melancholy,
Let him come and feast with me
    On the blithe face of my Polly.

With a fairy foot she dances
    On the green, the parson's daughter,
Like a sunbeam when it glances
    On the face of Cluny water;
Sweet as meadow hay in haytime,
    Fresh and fair as Christmas holly,
Light as birds that sing in Maytime
    Is the sweet young soul of Polly!

Scholars seek for bliss in books,
    Gray and dry, and bloodless wholly;
I peruse the rosy looks
    And the sunny smiles of Polly.
When she leaps with bounding glee,
    Like a trout in Cluny water,
All the soul of joy in me
    Flows to meet the parson's daughter.

Balls and parties make a din,
    Pleasure trips a sounding clatter,
But my triumph is to win
    A bright smile from the parson's daughter.
With much labour men prepare
    Pills to purge all melancholy,

I am wise to banish care
    With a single look at Polly.

When my heart is sick with babble
    Of the M.P.'s in the papers,
Where the Whig and Tory rabble
    Mad with faction cut their capers,
I, like bird that knows his nest
    On the banks of Cluny water,
Drown my sorrow on the breast
    Of the parson's blooming daughter.

Some will pant for money, some
    Posted high in public station,
Love with trumpet and with drum
    To parade before the nation;
Some will dice their lives away,
    Some with wine are wildly jolly,
But I am happy all the day,
    When I earn a kiss from Polly.

Who will show us any good?
    Look around and own your folly;
In your veins nurse kindly blood,
    And all you see is goodness wholly,

Nature loves the ruddy hue,
    Hates pale-blooded melancholy;
Somewhere grows a rose for you,
    As my rose I found in POLLY!

THE THREE GRACES

GOD hath three Graces that show forth his glory,
Ever repeated in life's wondrous story,
Youth, and Beauty, and Goodness, these three,
Charmed into one fair wonder in Thee,
                        Beautiful Dora!

YOUTH that comes fresh from the Lord of all glory,
Blushing with promise of life's fruitful story;
Sweet is the child that sings out with glee,
But sweeter is speech softly flowing from Thee,
                        Beautiful Dora!

BEAUTY, the vesture of God in creation,
From the light plumy fern to the strong starry nation,
Bright in the red rose, and bright in green tree,
But crowned with the bloom of all brightness in Thee,
                        Beautiful Dora!

GOODNESS that travels with blithe ministration,
In pulses of love through the veins of creation,
Unfetters the slave, and gives songs to the free,
And triumphs in largesses lavished by Thee,
Beautiful Dora!

YOUTH, and BEAUTY, and GOODNESS, three Graces,
Walk o'er the green Earth in blossomy places,
Each with the gift to her favourites free;
But blessed am I who have found all the three
In beautiful Dora!

AN APRIL SONG

My heart leaps up on a bright Spring day,
    When I look out to the sky,
And see the clouds in light display
    Floating gently by.
So was it, when I was a boy ;
    Now, though my hairs are gray,
My heart throbs with the self-same joy
    On a shining April day :
        Shine, shine, O April bright,
        And drive dull care away !

'Youth's the season made for joys,'
    An old song thus doth say,
But I can make a merry noise,
    Although my hairs are gray.
There's danger in youth's wild delights
    And hotly spurred desires ;

But safety dwells with sober sprights,
    And chastely glowing fires.
          Shine, shine, O April bright,
          And drive dull care away!

If thou wouldst earn a poet's thanks
    On a shining April day,
Oh, take me where the primrose prinks
    The gently sloping brae,
Where its sweet song the burnie purls
    Beneath the birchen spray,
And the fresh-sprouting leaf uncurls
    Its greenness to the day.
          Shine, shine, O April bright,
          And drive dull care away!

And let me hear the mavis pour
    His rich full-throated lay,
Unbosoming his redundant store
    Of gladness to the day;
And let me ban all moody thoughts
    To Limbo far away,
When all the air is quick with notes
    Of happy life to-day.
          Shine, shine, O April bright,
          And drive dull care away!

And let no breath invade my ear
    Of crude unreasoned babble,
And let no fretful word come near
    Of Whig and Tory squabble!
And, while on Pentland's grassy swell
    I weave my song with glee,
Let war with wrangling factions dwell;
    God's peace abides with me.
        Shine, shine, O April bright,
        And drive dull care away!

Right lovely is Thy world, O God,
    And I will praise it ever,
While I look up from earth's green sod
    To Thee, the General GIVER!
Thy grace did rein my youthful will,
    All strength to Thee belongs,
And Thou, when hairs are gray, dost fill
    The old man's breast with songs.
        Shine, shine, O April bright,
        And drive dull care away!

CUCKOO! CUCKOO!'

(Song for the First of May.)

'Cuckoo! cuckoo!' it haunts my way;
I hear that sweet note all the day,
From glen to glen, from brae to brae,
While I pursue my grassy way
    Through Ettrick vale and Yarrow!

'Cuckoo, cuckoo!' it still doth say,
The very spoken breath of May,
But viewless still from brae to brae,
As if a Spirit led my way,
    Through all the length of Yarrow!

How many a city drudge this day,
At large with me might sigh to stray,
Drinking deep draughts of breezy May,
With 'Cuckoo! cuckoo!' all the way,
    To hymn their march through Yarrow!

Poor city scribes! it makes me grieve
To think how ye from inky sleeve
And fretful quill find no reprieve,
Nor faction's babbling mart may leave
    To taste sweet May in Yarrow.

'Cuckoo! cuckoo!' it haunts my way,
Now here, now there, from brae to brae;
It floats and wanders with light play
From dark pine-wood to castle gray,
    And shepherd's cot in Yarrow!

Ye lords and ladies gay, who ride
Through London parks in dusty pride,
I wish you all might here abide,
With wimpling waters at your side,
    And cuckoo's note in Yarrow!

VACATION ODE

(Read at the end of the Winter Session of the Greek Classes, Edinburgh.)

    Ye sons of learned toil,
    Who with hard purpose moil
O'er grammar's thorny ways, and heaps of dusty tomes,
    Your posts are run. Be free,
    And with unchartered glee
Sport where the springy foot o'er lush green meadow roams!

    Not from the gaunt array
    Of mouldy parchments gray,
Drops the fine dew that slakes the knowledge-thirsting soul!
    But where from blade and spray
    Glances the fresh green May,
And rose-tipt flowerets blow, and lucid waters roll.

Rise, and no more be vext
From harsh disjointed text,
With learned strain to wrench the dubious-worded lore!
Up! and redeem your sight
With Heaven's broad-streaming light,
And pictured skies, and plains with beauty dappled o'er!

And let the genial note
That through green woods doth float
From viewless cuckoo, win your rapt ear's wise regard,
More than the cunning chime
Of curious-builded rhyme
From craft of smooth-lipped Greek, or deep-mouthed Roman bard.

Let roar of foaming floods,
And breath of growing woods,
Wave round you with more joy than flags of conquering kings!
Nor let your dull thought go
With painful pace and slow,

When every bursting grove with twittering gladness
rings!

Not wise who stern refuse
With gracious hand to use
The chance-sown sport, stray whim, and random-
started joy;
In many a shifting mood,
With gamesome lustihood,
Quaint Nature respite finds from life's severe employ.

You to familiar halls
A father's voice recalls,
And tells your virtues' roll with broad benignant pride;
While eager at the gate
A mother's love doth wait
To gain her laurelled boy back to her careful side.

And troops of sisters fair,
Whose smiles make blithe the air,
And rings of lusty boys, with merry sun-brown faces,
These wait your skill to guide
Their steps by mountain side,
To lone green glens remote, and strange old castled
places!

      Now home! You need no goad
      From me on such a road ;
Your native steam will urge this taskless travel duly ;
      And may God love you so,
      Your strength through weal and woe,
As I did love you well, and strove to serve you truly!

PASTEUR'S WORD TO YOUNG MEN

J'ai toujours aimé la jeunesse. Du plus, loin qu'il me souvienne dans ma vie d'homme, je ne crois pas avoir jamais abordé un étudiant sans lui dire ; travaille et persévere. Le travail amuse et seul il profite à l'homme, au citoyen, à la patrie.

BRACE up your wills, brave-hearted boys,
To mingle hardship with your joys,
    In life's abundant measure ;
Put hand to plough, and persevere,
When skies are dark, when skies are clear,
For labour is the title here
    That gives a claim to pleasure.

Who's he that feeds his soul with fears,
And makes sweet luxury of tears,
    And cradles dainty sorrow ;
At every breath of harm who frets,
And grumbles when his shoes he wets,
And on a rainy day forgets
    That suns will shine to-morrow ?

Where would he live? In some soft spot,
Where all things can for all be got,
    Without or toil or trouble!
What sport were this, with nothing hard
To do, no hindrance to retard,
No risk to run, and one reward
    For all—a floating bubble!

Leave dreams to fools! The name of Life
Is work—a various-mingled strife
    Of Powers that slumber never;
The swelling seas, the circling spheres,
The racing winds, the rolling years,
The fateful tide of hopes and fears,
    Work bravely on for ever.

Work you with them, all work with God,
His tools to stir the teeming sod,
    Or load the fruitful river;
And, if it chance His work we mar,
With limping faith, or loveless war,
His touch to music turns the jar,
    With strength that faileth never.

Trench deep the soil; cast broad the seeds,
And branching trees o'er noxious weeds
      Will spread their fruitful measure.
Put hand to plough, and persevere,
When skies are dark, when skies are clear;
For labour is the relish here
      That gives a zest to pleasure!

THE STUDENT'S FAREWELL TO SUMMER

I HEARD the whistling North wind say
    When it came down with power,
Athwart the russet ferny brae,
    And by the old gray tower:
I heard the whistling North wind say
    Bright Summer suns no more
Shall shine on Oban's dimpled bay,
    And green Dunolly's shore.

I saw a fox-glove in the dell
    Beneath the crag so gray,
One lonely, lean, belated bell,
    And thus it seemed to say:
The glory of the June is past,
    My purple kin are gone,
And I am left a poor outcast
    To die in the cold alone!

I saw the long black ragged cloud
  O'ercap the frowning Bens,
And trails of thick blue mist enshroud
  The green far-gleaming glens ;
And thus the black cloud seemed to say,
  Now Summer suns are dim,
The stern old Winter holds his sway,
  And I will reign with him.

And is it so ?—brightest of things,
  God's beauty-vested Summer,
Shall it depart on hasty wings
  That was so late a comer?
And I who lived with fragrant breeze,
  Blue skies and purple braes,
On hueless flowers and leafless trees
  Must feed my widowed gaze?

It may not be : up! let us go!
  I will not stay and look
Where gorgeous Nature's pictured show
  Is now a blotted book.
Let Nature die! She'll live again
  When six dull months expire ;

H

Meanwhile against both wind and rain
    Heap we the blazing fire

Snug in the chambered town! and call
    Our troop of friends together,
And for six months let no word fall
    Of Nature, wind or weather;
And ply the work of thought or art
    That helps both self and neighbour,
And sing with glad and guileless heart
    The song that seasons labour!

And bring the gray tomes from our shelves
    And learn strong will from Cato,
And take high value of ourselves
    From lofty-thoughted Plato:
And, while with friendly cheer we pass
    The rare, rich-blooded bottle,
Give learned flavour to the glass
    By saws from Aristotle!

And then we'll talk of Church and State,
    And wish the hangman's rope
To wed their necks to righteous Fate
    Who love the Roman Pope!

And blame the loons who gave the sway
    To the mere polled majority,
With clamorous yells to overbray
    The voice of grave authority.

And then,—why then, we'll go to bed,
    And wake, above all sorrow
Of factious brawls to lift our head,
    By faithful work to-morrow,
Work through long weeks of blustering storm,
    And Winter's gloomy reign,
Till the great pulse of things grows warm,
    And Nature lives again ;

And suns shall shine, and birds shall sing,
    And odorous breezes blow,
And ferns uncurl their folded wing
    Where star-eyed flow'rets grow ;
And surly blasts shall cease to bray,
    And stormy seas to roar
On Oban's warm sun-fronting bay,
    And green Dunolly's shore.

A SONG OF GOOD COUNSEL

(TO YOUNG MEN)

German Air—'Geniesst den Reitz des Lebens.'

BRAVE boys, would you live wisely,
    To God and Nature true,
Hear me, and I precisely
    Will tell you what to do.

This world's no place for weaving
    Light webs of fancies grand,
But for firm will achieving
    High purpose with strong hand.

If weaklings deem it cruel
    That life so hard should be,
Deem thou all hard things fuel
    For victories meant for thee!

A SONG OF GOOD COUNSEL

March on, and never weary,
    With firm and steady pace ;
But like the lark be cheery,
    And skyward turn thy face.

Who frets prolongs his sorrow,
    Who fears makes strong his foe,
And double woe to-morrow
    From golden dreams will flow.

Nor dream nor doubt, but stoutly
    The task that nearest lies
Perform, and wait devoutly
    On God, who helps the wise.

He helps no fools, and rightly
    Lays vauntful sinners low,
Who hold the helm not tightly
    When windy passions blow.

And evermore in danger,
    With gleesome faith be strong ;
The devil remains a stranger
    To breasts that teem with song.

And never in thy daring
   Dare for thyself alone,
But with thy brother sharing
   The good that's most thine own.

And own the God who sent thee
   On life's wide sea to swim,
And this glad being lent thee
   To live and work with Him.

A SONG OF BACKGAMMON

Take my word for't, this game is not
  A blind unreasoned rattle,
Where any fool with random shot
  May gain a brainless battle;
But 'tis a game that you must play
  With all your wits about you,
Or for your folly sharply pay
  When evil Fate shall flout you!

Life too's a game, I tell you true,
  Of mingled skill and chances,
Which each brave heart must play anew
  With men and circumstances.
'Tis Providence that throws the dice,
  Our function not to choose them,
But with quick glance, and measure nice,
  And venture bold to use them.

A game like that strategic game
    Which makes the soldier's story,
Where chance does much for praise or blame,
    But skill doth reap the glory.
You know your ground, you know your foe:
    Advancing or retreating,
You choose the moment when the blow
    Will give the bloodiest greeting.

Five points there be which you must know
    This noble game to carry,
First make your own men forward go,
    Then block your adversary;
Then let no straggler loosely stand
    Alone and unprotected,
But still be nigh with helping hand,
    Where harm may be suspected.

And never pile your men with waste
    Of supererogation,
But spread them well, adroitly placed
    At each convenient station;
And chiefly keep your chequer strong,
    That, when with happy venture

You snap your foeman up, he long
    May wait the chance to enter.

And now I've told you how to play
    At life and at backgammon,
As true as ever in his day
    Spake that Egyptian Ammon;
And, if you use my rule aright,
    In life you'll be a winner;
If not, you'll die in woeful plight,
    Like many an unwhipt sinner.

A SONG FOR THE ROAD, AND A RULE FOR THE LIFE

A SONG for the road, and a rule for the life,
    Receive from a lusty old man, Tom ;
Fear God, and march on, and make war to the knife,
    When the enemy crosses your plan, Tom.
For life's a campaign ; then foot it apace,
    There are dangers enough in your track, Tom ;
Still keep a sharp out-look, and show a bold face,
    Or the foe will be soon on your back, Tom !
        For this is true wisdom, I wish you to know,
        Sail close to the wind when you tack, Tom !
        We live, while we live, by the pluck that we show,
        And if we don't stand, we must flee from the foe,
        And fall with a stab in the back, Tom !

You see yon huge Ben that runs up to the sky,
    So ruggedly grand and sublime, Tom ;

A staircase so steep, you think, would defy
  The cat o' the mountain to climb, Tom!
But, 'tis all a delusion—just wisely survey
  With your eye, and then take it aslant, Tom,
And you'll find what they say, that you can't find a way,
  Is a tissue of cowardly cant, Tom.
    For this, etc.

The worst of all words in the language is—*But*,
  For whatever you purpose or plan, Tom,
This weak monosyllable comes in to cut
  The sinews that make you a man, Tom.
'Tis noble to dare, *but* not pleasant at all
  A lion to meet, where you fare, Tom;
It may suit you to ride, *but* a rider may fall,
  So you sit and you rot in your chair, Tom.
    For this, etc.

Some people's devotion delights in this notion
  Of heaven, that when we get there, Tom,
We'll have nothing to do but to float in the blue,
  And pipe a psalm tune in the air, Tom!
If 'tis so in the sky, we shall know by and by,
  But on earth 'tis much otherwise now, Tom,

Where the battle we fight brings a keener delight
    Than the laurels we wear on the brow, Tom.
        For this, etc.

The end of all living is simply to live,
    Is what Aristotle would say, Tom ;
And form to the formless by labour to give
    Is to live the most excellent way, Tom !
A moth in the sunbeam may flutter an hour,
    To flutter is all that it can, Tom ;
But to fashion great thoughts into deeds is the dower
    God gave to high-reasoning man, Tom !
        For this, etc.

If you shrink from no danger where valour avails,
    There's nothing can stand in your way, Tom ;
You may start, like stout Lincoln, a splitter of rails,
    And be king of the people some day, Tom.
The Romans were lords of the sea and the land,
    And what was the reason of that, Tom ?
At the word of command, they marched on sword in hand,
    And they laid all their enemies flat, Tom.
        For this, etc.

My sermon is done—still rejoice in the toils
    That the travel of life may attend, Tom.
Put foot after foot; never number the miles;
    You will know when you come to the end, Tom!
Fear God; every atom takes rank at His call;
    For the world is no rope of sand, Tom;
Link hangs upon link; and 'tis profit to all
    That each march at the word of command, Tom.
        For this is true wisdom, I wish you to know,
        Sail close to the wind when you tack, Tom!
        We live, while we live, by the pluck that we show,
        And if we don't stand, we must flee from the foe,
        And fall with a stab in the back, Tom!

BENEDICITE

German Air—'Alles Schweige!'

Angels holy,
High and lowly,
Sing the praises of the Lord!
Earth and sky, all living nature,
Man, the stamp of thy Creator,
Praise ye, praise ye, God the Lord!

Sun and moon bright,
Night and noonlight,
Starry temples azure-floored,
Cloud and rain, and wild winds' madness
Sons of God that shout for gladness,
Praise ye, praise ye, God the Lord!

Ocean hoary,
Tell his glory,

Cliffs where tumbling seas have roared!
Pulse of waters blithely beating,
Wave advancing, wave retreating,
Praise ye, praise ye, God the Lord!

    Rock and high land,
    Wood and island,
Crag where eagle's pride hath soared,
Mighty mountains purple-breasted,
Peaks cloud-cleaving, snowy-crested,
Praise ye, praise ye, God the Lord,

    Rolling river
    Praise him ever,
From the mountain's deep vein poured;
Silver fountain clearly gushing,
Troubled torrent madly rushing,
Praise ye, praise ye, God the Lord!

    Bond and free man,
    Land and sea man,
Earth with peoples widely stored,
Woodman lone o'er prairies ample,
Full-voiced choir in costly temple,
Praise ye, praise ye, God the Lord!

Praise him ever,
Bounteous Giver!
Praise him, father, friend, and Lord!
Each glad soul its free course winging,
Each blithe voice its free song singing,
Praise the great and mighty Lord!

HYMN

Air—'Belmont.'

O FOR a heart from self set free,
    And doubt and fret, and care,
Light as a bird, instinct with glee,
    That fans the breezy air!

O for a mind whose virtue moulds
    All sensuous fair display,
And, like a strong commander, holds
    A world of thoughts in sway!

O for an eye that's clear to see,
    A hand that waits on Fate,
To pluck the ripe fruit from the tree,
    And never comes too late!

O for a life with firm-set root,
  And breadth of leafy green,
And flush of blooming wealth, and fruit
  That glows with mellow sheen!

O for a death from sharp alarms
  And bitter memories free:
A gentle death in God's own arms,
  Whose dear Son died for me!

A SONG OF OLD AGE

Sing me a song of old age,
    When the blood no longer is boiling,
When heaviness drags the limbs,
    And the arm is wearied with toiling.

Not to the blare of the trump,
    Loud wars, and masterful slaughters;
But sing me a song of sweet peace,
    To the hum of low-murmuring waters.

Sing me a song where I sit,
    Where the breath of summer is blowing,
And, dappled with vegetive gold,
    The soft, green grass is growing.

Sing me a song on the skirt
    Of the brown far-stretching mountain,
Where the birch-tree droops
    O'er the trickling grace of the fountain;

Where roses, the white and the red,
    Like happy sisters together,
Ramble up hill and down dale,
    And spread their smiles to the weather.

Sing me a song of old age,
    Not wildly and wantonly sweeping
Over the limits of sense,
    With proud self-confident leaping;

Not in a thunder-car
    With Jove's red lightning flaring,
Measuring measureless space
    With thoughts that revel in daring.

But sing me a song like the brook
    That through the green lea wanders
From grassy bend to bend,
    With lightly twined meanders;

A song of homeliest things,
    Familiar, fond, and common,
Wild flowers, eyes of children,
    And smiles of gracious woman;

Things that gently slide,
    In hours of happy musing,
Into the home of thought
    Without the pain of choosing.

Sing of the time when men
    Looked forth on the young creation,
Young and fresh with wonder, and love,
    And strong veneration ;

Feeling the might of the gods
    Who with glory and terror confound us,
Weaving a mystical chain
    Of sleepless miracles round us ;

Stirring our hearts with thoughts
    That kinship claim with the Highest,
Laying us low with a word
    When the voice goes forth—*Thou diest !*

Sing me a song of the time
    When hymns and songs were the teachers,
And sun, and moon, and stars
    Were God's own bright-eyed preachers.

Better to worship the spheres
    As they wheel their courses benignly
Than nothing in nature to own
    That works with wisdom divinely.

Better to worship the streams
    With bounty exuberant flowing,
Than toil in a blind machine
    Nor love nor liberty knowing.

Sing me a song of repose
    That delights in worship and wonder,
Feeling a God in the bloom
    Of the flower, and the roll of the thunder.

Sing me a song of the Sabbath
    When the cares of the hour are sleeping,
And toilsome mortals bright feast
    Of hope for the future are keeping;

A song of the general Church,
    Where rich and poor together
Pray 'neath a gilded dome,
    Or on slope of the purple heather.

There in memory mild
  Let the patriarch families gather,
Circling with me the throne
  Of the great all-bountiful Father.

Names of hoary renown
  That blazon the roll of the ages,
Warriors, kings, and statesmen,
  Poets, and prophets, and sages,

Men, the leaders of men,
  The wise, the valiant-hearted,
Who marched in glory through life,
  And in trails of glory departed.

These I would have while I live
  For guidance and fellowship near me;
These when I die with words
  Of proved old wisdom to cheer me!

Give me—oh, give me, dear God!
  Nor power, nor honour, nor riches,
Nor pomp and splendour of life,
  That dazzles the crowd and bewitches:

But give me the words of the wise,
    And the smiles of earth's beautiful daughters,
To weave me a song of old age
    By the hum of low-murmuring waters.

II

SONNETS

RELIGION

I

WHAT is religion? I will tell you what
   I think it is: not blindly to disown
Thy reason, and to crouch and lay thee flat
   Before a something terrible unknown;
Not girt with bristling fence of marshalled creeds
   To thunder bans from high-presumptuous throne,
Nor with the mumbled charm of counted beads
   To bring down God, and make your will His own:
But in God's face with reverent love to look
   Here where it shines in sky and land and sea,
And, where a Prophet spake in holy book,
   To hear his word, and take the truth to thee,
And hold it fast, and tread earth's lowly sod
With lofty soul, as one that walks with God.

II

WHAT is religion? Good my friend, as lust
   Tricked out like love, drags white souls through
      the mire,
Hateful, that heaven's light-winged ethereal fire
Dimmed with dun smoke is blurred, or choked with
      dust;
And as sometimes, where men are drunk with wine,
   At the stale ending of a sumptuous feast,
   Who more than man was mighty, less than beast
Lies reft of reason, bedded with the swine:
   Even so religion, best of things when good,
When bad is worst. To own His sovereign law,
   Who reins the spheres will brace thy manful mood;
But, if thou kiss the sod in abject awe,
   And nurse crude dreams in fearful fancy's school,
   Religion is a ghost, and thou a fool.

THE TRINITY

If there be three in one and one in three
    In the Divine perfection, then may Man,
Made in God's image, with wise reverence see
    Some mirrored hint of this tri-unal plan
In his small type of being; and I find
    Three forces which to blissful issue lead,
In all the strivings of our human kind,
    To spur their progress, or to help their need.
First stands the THOUGHT, the father-force which brings
    Shape from the shapeless with imperial sway,
Then comes the WORD, born of the Thought, which wings
    Far East, far West, its proud prophetic way;
And then the SPIRIT that arms with trenchant power
The elect man, whose DEED commands the hour.

CHRIST AND CHRISTENDOM

If Jesus came, and walked the Earth to-morrow,
    What would He say to many things we do
Here in this England, where His name we borrow
    To test the false coin, and to stamp the true?
What would He say to our blown speculations,
    Slowness to love, and hot haste to be rich,
Gilded parades, self-trumpeting ovations,
    Folly high-throned, and wisdom in the ditch?
What to our churches, catechisms, creeds,
    That murder peace, and set the world aflame,
Begodded wafers, crosses, relics, beads,
    Sense conjured into nonsense in God's name?
I know not; but I know well who would say,
'*This Jew suits not the England of to-day!*'

ATHEISTIC SCIENTISTS

There is a sort of men whose faith is all
    In their five fingers, and what fingering brings,
With all beyond of wondrous great and small,
    Unnamed, uncounted in their tale of things;
A race of blinkards, who peruse the case
    And shell of life, but feel no soul behind,
And in the marshalled world can find a place
    For all things, only not the marshalling Mind.
'Tis strange, 'tis sad; and yet why blame the mole
    For channelling earth?—such earthy things are they.
E'en let them muster forth in blank array,
Frames with no pictures, pictures with no soul,
    I, while this dædal dome o'erspans the sod,
    Will own the builder's hand, and worship God.

CRITICISM

Μὴ κρίνετε ἵνα μὴ κριθῆτε.

If you are young, and wish to air your pinion;
   If you know little and would seem to know
Much: if to listen to your crude opinion,
   Echoed tenfold where every wind may blow,
Tickles your ears, and lends stilts to your pride,
   Then be a critic: you might gain a penny
In some less honest way; and you will guide
   At your blind will the blind, unthinking many.
But, would you cherish in your faithful breast
   The seed of truth, and by that virtue grow
To manhood's bravest stature with the best,
   Judge not: but look with love and reverence low—
Just homage of the lesser to the greater—
On God's two-fronted image—LIFE and NATURE!

SUBJECTIVE AND OBJECTIVE.

THERE is a sort of men that open wide
    The portals of their soul to Nature's lessons;
And in their audience-chamber dwells the pride
    Of things extern in finely-chased impressions.
Another sort I know, that, like a tide,
    Roll on with swelling breast, and towering crest,
And with a tyrannous bounty override
    All base confronters. Well; which sort is best?
Each kind is good; for both God hath his use,
    Who takes for stepping-stones, or wields as tools
    The schemes of sages, and the dreams of fools;
Opposing forces to one end conduce;
    But they to God most kinship do approve,
Who see things as they are, and see all things with
    love.[1]

[1] What Goethe said of the Frau von Stein.

TO SCOTCH HERESY-HUNTERS

'No! you must change your tactics; you may never
    Make full-grown breasts breathe free in baby-bonds;
The stream of thinking flows on like a river,
    And you would dam it up in village ponds!
Good friends, take my advice, I love you well;
    Creeds did their duty bravely in their day;
Primers that taught the clever boy to spell,
    Who now looks up, and in free, manly way
Explores his Bible. Why did Luther fling
    His ban against the Pope and his misdeeds,
    If private judgment must be caged in creeds,
Each free word gagged, and clipt each upward wing,
    And you with churchly ban, and pulpit drum,
    Strike Bible-readers blind and prophets dumb!

THE ORIGIN OF EVIL

THE origin of Evil?—good my friend,
  Ask him who helps my vegetable needs,
  The gardener there, the origin of weeds;
He'll turn about and stare to comprehend
  What thing you mean. The buds, he deems, are
    there,
No doubt with very proper right to grow;
  And he with them has equal right to care
For flowery fragrance, and for blooming show.
  This man is wise; and you, what thing are you?
A thing of idle dreams and fancies crude:
Evil exists that you may make it good,
  Else had the saints on earth scant work to do.
What would you have? in Paradise no doubt
Weeds grandly grew, and Adam plucked them out.

THE ORIGIN OF EVIL

The origin of Evil?—good my friend,
    To ask such questions proves thee far from wise;
    No mightiest man that walks beneath the skies
Hath plumb to measure, or device to mend
The vasty universe. If thou would'st know
    Whence Evil comes, say first what evil means,
    And if this pictured pomp of shifting scenes
Which men call life, a many-mingling show,
    Was made for your mere pleasure or for mine.
Cease foolish questions; here for me and you
Close by our door is fruitful work to do;
    Accept the task, and own the work divine;
Sow, plant, or build, drain fields or cleave the clod,
But spend no breath in arguing with God.

ΘΕΛΩ, ΘΕΛΩ ΜΑΝΗΝΑΙ

(To Mrs. J. W.)

'*I will, I will be mad!*' so some one cried,
    And wisely, if with the right kind of madness;
But not all surging seas are safe to ride,
    And some ripe fruits rot quickly into badness.
Some mad with women loved a fair she-devil,
    Some mad with God to stocks and stones did bend,
Some mad with learning span their brains in drivel,
    Some mad with wine have murdered their best friend.
But art thou mad, as one I know, to fling
    Bounties and blessings with wide arms abroad,
To lift the low, and teach the sad to sing,
    And bring the outcast sinner back to God,
Such madness, like the rich redundant Nile,
The more it floods the banks, the more makes fat the soil.

WAR

(To a Quaker.)

FRIEND, God has many sides. Deem not that war
  Which throws the bloody dice for priests and kings
Is Devil-born or Devil-sent, to mar
  The fair-proportioned harmony of things.
All things are full of war; not only man,
  But earth and air and waters in their flowing
Have their rude jostlings, which disturb the plan
  That peaceful souls would map out for their going.
For why? The strife of battling forces strains
  Each virtue to its top of hardihood;
The weaker falls; more strength the stronger gains,
  And fruitful fatness grows from fields of blood.
So mighty trees from wrestling with the storms,
Rise to more pride, and spread their giant arms.

OUTSIDE AND INSIDE

(A Sketch from High Life.)

BEHOLD this mansion how proud-perched it stands
   Mid old ancestral woods and grassy meads,
   And cradled lakelets, where the sea-gull breeds,
And leafy prospect o'er far seas and lands;
And, while thine eye feasts on this lordly scene,
   Belike the thought doth through thy fancy fare,
   'How happy I, had I been born the heir
To this proud palace, and this broad demesne!'
Foolish! for hear; behind this goodly show
   Vice holds her conclave, Folly keeps her school;
Pride piles the top stone; Ruin digs below;
   The lord's a gambler, and his mate a fool;
The son lies tremulous with the drunkard's doom,
The daughter last night ran off with the groom.

SICKNESS AND RECOVERY

I.—Sickness.

As when a sea-gull, customed long to sweep
    With breezy range from shimmering sea to sea,
    In revelry of wafture fair and free,
O'er the broad bosom of the boundless deep;
Him now an idle boy, after a storm,
    Hath caught, and pruned his wing, and closely barred
    All outlet from the farmer's narrow yard,
Where he must hop about from worm to worm,
A sorry sight to see. So me, once king
    Of thoughts far-stretching, and far-wandering ways,
Mischance hath caught, and clipt my venturous wing,
    And chained me to a round of deedless days,
With all life's organ-hymns of high desire
Sunk to the creakings of a broken lyre!

II.—Recovery.

There now, thou faithless heart, learn once again
   To doubt thyself, and put thy trust in GOD,
   Whose virtue breathes live breath into the clod,
And with a touch lures forth a golden vein
Of joy from sadness! When one dismal blot
   Mars the blue sky, and wraps the day in night,
Is the sun dead, for that thy little spot
   Glooms for an hour, uncheered by kindly light?
O fool! fool! fool! as soon may craft of man
   Dry up the swelling founts that richly pour
From the broad flanks of Nevis Ben, as span
   The breadth of blessing GOD doth keep in store
For whom He loves. His nature is to give,
Thine to receive; this truth believe, and live.

ROBERT BURNS

I

(The bright side; on seeing his statue recently erected on the Thames Embankment, London.)

WELL done, my little Scotland! out of five
   In statued state that look forth on the Thames,[1]
Thou countest two in London's mighty hive,
   Conspicuous planted with her noblest names.
Oxford breeds scholars, Scotland thinkers: so
   Learning from logic borrowed curious skill,
And grateful Thames received in marble show
   With stamp from Oxford, subtle-thoughted Mill.

---

[1] Besides Burns, John Stuart Mill, Tyndall, the translator of the Bible, Brunelle, the engineer of the Thames Tunnel, and Raikes, the founder of the great evangelical organism of Sabbath schools. The variety of types represented in this marble pentarchy is highly characteristic of the Catholicity of feeling bred in such an omnifarious capital as London; and it certainly must be looked on as one of the greatest compliments ever paid to the Scottish intellect, that the same writer should receive honour in England both as a logical authority in the court of academic honours, and as a political philosopher in the streets of the busy metropolis.

And now another Scot, strong, fiery-souled,
    Finds honoured station on this famous strand,
Whose soulful song with swelling virtue rolled
    From heart to heart to each remotest land,
And every Grace bowed low, and Phoebus smiled
Where unschooled Nature led her lusty child.

II

(The dark side ; on making a careful study of the Life of Burns.)

Poor Burns! I may not sing a song to thee,
    For tears creep o'er me, when I ope thy book,
To think what jars of sorrow marred thy glee,
    What fogs of folly dimmed thy starry look!
Not mine to weigh thy sin, or sound thy shame,
    But I must pity where I cannot praise;
No wash of smooth-lipped words can wipe the blame
    Thine own confession heaped upon thy ways.
Poor child of whim, with wide-dispredden sails
    Unballasted, unpiloted, thou gave
Thy plunging bark, the sport of every gale,
    To drift at random o'er the treacherous wave;
Nor knew to shape thy course, and hold thy plan,
And show how much of God may dwell in MAN!

CARLYLE

Thou wert a Titan, but a Titan tossed
    With wild tumultuous heavings in thy breast,
And fancy-fevered, and cool judgment lost
    In mighty maelstroms of divine unrest.
What souls were drugged with doubt in sceptic time
    Thy cry disturbed into believing life,
And fools that raved in prose or writhed in rhyme
    Were sharply surgeoned by thy needful knife:
But, if there were who in this storm of things
    Sighed for sweet calm, and in this dark for light,
And in this jar for the wise Muse that sings
    All wrong into the ordered ranks of right,
They thanked not thee, who didst assault their brain
With thunder-claps and water-spouts for rain.

THE LATE REV. DR. NORMAN MACLEOD

(Written on reading his life by the Rev. Dr. Donald Macleod, Glasgow.)

As when a man, a weary-footed wight,
   Tramping long leagues of waste and wintry road,
Sudden uplooks, and recreates his sight
   With novel prospect, bursting bright and broad,
Of yellow field, and green soft-gleaming glen,
   And rolling stream, and wide rich-waving wood,
And purple brae, and blue embosomed Ben,
   And shining crest of laughter-loving flood:
So I, lean traveller, through gray land of books,
   Where weeds are rank, and foodful fruits are few,
With ampler thought uprose and brighter looks,
   When thy brave life, great teacher, flashed in view;
And launched my skiff, and caught a gale from thee,
Like a young sailor on a broad blue sea!

SYDNEY DOBELL

(On hearing of his death.)

AND thou too gone! One more bright soul away
    To swell the mighty sleepers 'neath the sod.
One less to honour and to love, and say,
    Who lives with thee doth live half-way to God.
My chaste-souled Sydney! Thou wert carved too fine
    For coarse observance of the general eye:
But who might look into thy soul's fair shrine
    Saw bright gods there, and felt their presence nigh.
Oh, if we owe warm thanks to Heaven, 'tis when
    In the slow progress of the struggling years
Our touch is blessed to feel the pulse of men
    Who walk in love and light above their peers
White-robed, and forward point with guiding hand,
Breathing a heaven around them where they stand.

CHINESE GORDON

I

'I WANT a hero'—well, that wish is wise ;
    Who hath no hero lives not near to God ;
For heroes are the steps by which we rise
    To reach His hand who lifts us from the sod.
I'll give you one. You've heard of Chinese Gordon,
    Who laid the hot-brained pig-tail rebel low,
Strong, shod with peace or with sharp-bladed sword on,
    To gain an ally or to crush a foe,
    And reap respect from both. How came it so ?
He used no magic, and he owned no spell,
    But with keen glance, strong will, and weighty blow,
Did one thing at a time, and did it well ;
    And sought no praise from men, as in God's eye,
    Nobly to live content or nobly die.

CHINESE GORDON

II

SOME men live near to God, as my right arm
    Is near to me; and thus they walk about
Mailed in full proof of faith, and bear a charm
    That mocks at fear, and bars the door on doubt,
And dares the impossible. So Gordon, thou,
    Through the hot stir of this distracted time,
Dost hold thy course, a flaming witness how,
    To do and dare, and make our lives sublime
As God's campaigners. What live we for but this,
    Into the sour to breathe the soul of sweetness,
    The stunted growth to rear to fair completeness,
Drown sneers in smiles, kill hatred with a kiss,
    And to the sandy waste bequeath the fame
    That the grass grew behind us where we came!

ALEXANDER PEDEN

(Written at his grave under the twin thorn trees, Cumnock.)

HERE let me stand beneath the sacred shade
   Of these twin thorns that shield a prophet's bones!
   I have stood high on monumental stones,
Where Memphian kings august made grand parade,
Not moved as here. My loves are with the braves
   Who stand erect for freedom and for right,
   When rampant pride, harsh law, and sworded might
Would crush out thought, and stamp all men for
     slaves;
And such was Peden. In the day when kings
   Claimed right divine to murder honest men,
And venal bishops flapped their vulture wings
   O'er God's dear saints, hounded from glen to glen,
Peden stood firm; and to his faith then shown
We owe that now we call our souls our own.

TO THE RIGHT HONOURABLE THE BARONESS BURDETT COUTTS

To gather gold is a wide-customed game,
    To Scot, or Greek, or subtle Hebrew free;
But how to spend it, and to gather fame
    By spending, Angela, we learn from thee.
God is a Giver; and most like to God
    Whose heart doth lend his hand most large employ;
Even as the Sun who flings his light abroad,
    Far East, far West, and where he shines is joy.
Good Lady, as I love the Sun's blest ray,
    So I love thee, so bland, benign, and clear,
And of pure sweetness redolent, like the May
    Breathing rich essence of the flowery year;
And all the good within me owns thy sway,
    And all the bad is not, when thou art near!

TO THE RIGHT HONOURABLE THE EARL OF ROSEBERY

(On hearing his admirable Rectorial Address on Scottish patriotism.)

WELL, here at last God sends a Lord who dares
   To be a Scot, and knows to be a man,
And on broad breast of honour proudly wears
   The bristling badge that stamps the Scottish clan.
There are who live on Scottish ground ashamed
   Of their Scotch blood, and with light foreign wares
Tinker their lack-wit brains, politely tamed
   To hold the skirt up of a type not theirs
In servile sequence. Not so this brave Lord
   Hangs from his country and his kinship loose,
But stands where God him planted, with bright sword
   In hand, like Knox, for native Scottish use,
And Renwick, high-souled boy, whose noble crime
Rang out the reign of lies, an hour before the time.[1]

---

[1] James Renwick, the last of the illustrious band of Scottish martyrs and patriots, suffered execution at the Grassmarket of Edinburgh on the 17th February 1688, at the early age of 26 years. To this noble army of martyrs, more than to any other cause—however some persons may seem willing to forget it—Scotland owes the passion for ecclesiastical and political freedom, which our English politicians, made of less stubborn materials, have sometimes found it difficult to comprehend.

DEAN RAMSAY

(late of St. John's, Edinburgh, on the Publication of the Twentieth Edition of his book, *Reminiscences of Scottish Life and Character.*)

HAIL! wreathed in smiles, thou genial book! and hail
   Who wove thy web of bright and various hue,
The wise old man, who gleaned the social tale
   And thoughtful jest and roguish whim that grew
Freely on Scotland's soil, when Scotland knew
   To be herself, nor lusted to assume
   Smooth English ways—that they might live and bloom
With freshness, ever old and ever new,
   In human hearts. Thrice happy he who knows
With sportive light the cloudy thought to clear,
   And round his head the playful halo throws
That plucks the terror from the front severe :
   Such grace was thine, and such thy gracious part,
Thou wise old Scottish man of large and loving heart.

DR. WALTER SMITH

(On hearing him preach a sermon on Isaiah xi. 13, applied to the relations of Great Britain and Ireland.)

THANK God! here comes at last a man who knows
    What Bible means; not one who speaks on Sunday
What serves the hour, as men don Sunday clothes,
    But bravely leaps into the march of Monday
With Sunday texts. Deem'st thou the Saviour meant
    To brew weak gospel for a sickly nation
Dreaming of Heaven, when groaning Earth up sent
    A cry for swift and sharp regeneration?
Not so; believe His spoken word: I came,
    Not peace to give my people, but a sword;
Love may not league with Power enthroned on shame,
    Nor Truth shake hands with falsehood most abhorred;
My Truth invades the world, and in my creed
Each word walks forth in mail, and means a deed.

ROBERT LEE

(An accomplished Edinburgh clergyman and Professor of Biblical Criticism, who was put under ban by the General Assembly for his defence of the freedom of Ritual in the Scottish Church.)

Prophets are few; and these so few, oh shame!
  When they are here, we vex with wordy wars,
  Heap them with lies, grave their fair front with scars,
And lay them low in death, bleeding with blame,
And gashed with rude reproach. Such fate was thine,
  Far-thoughted Lee, above thy people wise,
  Who didst o'ershoot the range of vulgar eyes,
And with thy life didst pay the noble fine
Which wisdom pays, when folly acts the lord.
  We wept; but now 'neath a disclouded sky,
Cleared by thy martyr death, free praise is poured.
  'Twas meet that for the people one should die;
Death smothers hate; and, when the wise man dies,
Even fools begin to dream of being wise.

LONDON

If thou art one grown big in home conceit,
    A village oracle, a parish god,
Where every dangler in the sleepy street
    Reflects thy fancies and subserves thy nod,
Cease with thy mirrored self well pleased to dwell;
    Come forth, and prove thy mettle in the strife,
And let huge London's billowy tumult tell
    The unvalued cheapness of thy twinkling life!
Titanic London! wonder of the world,
    Thyself a world, and, like the world, a flow
Of powers with such vortiginous vastness whirled
    Seems a blind rush, sans law, sans rule; but no!
The mighty mass throbs with one common soul,
And unseen gods inform the heaving whole.

ENGLAND

(Lines written on returning from a tour in Italy.)

ALL hail, brave land of cloud, and mist, and smoke,
    England with all thy blots I love thee well,
For thou hast thews of iron, heart of oak,
    And mettle to defy all fiends in hell;
Grand drift of Time; the traffic of old Tyre,
    The soldier-strength, the statesman-craft of Rome,
Fine Greekish lore, and sacred Hebrew fire,
    'Neath thy gray sky have found a friendly home.
Let others train the peach, and trim the vine,
    And breathe more sweetly more luxurious air;
    Greatly to plan, and gallantly to dare,
And yoke harsh Nature to thy car be thine!
    Thank God, who, for defect of gentler charm,
    Gave thee strong brain, firm will, and weighty arm!

THE SAVOY

Wise was Charles Lamb, who in the busy Strand
    Saw the full tide of life and wept for joy,
Nor less whose quiet thought can understand
    To sum the ages in the still Savoy,
As I sit here, and muse the hours away,
    And call up placid ghosts of mighty men,
Who made a thunderous tumult in their day,
    And spoke brave words that shook big kingdoms
        then ;
Where are they now ? I'd give a thousand pound
    To hold short parley with that John of Gaunt,
    Or with Dan Chaucer weave an old Romaunt,
Or rhyme with Douglas in this hallowed ground ;
    It may not be ; but what they did I know ;
    They cleared the soil, and sowed the seed ; we grow.

TO HIS GRACE THE DUKE OF ARGYLL

On the fair marge of the far-winding flood
    Rises a stately castellated pile,
Fenced by huge Bens, and with rich wealth of wood
    Festooned and fringed for many a rambling mile:
It is the palace-home of the Argyll:
    Pass it not lightly by: it wears a name
Shall warm the heart of grateful Scotland, while
    Knox and the Bruce shall swell the trump of fame.
Happy the nation which, when kings conspire
    To quench the flame they should be proud to fan,
Hath high-souled leaders strong to scorn the hire
    That tempts the courtier to betray the man:
Leaders like those who fathered thine and thee,
Thou wise Argyll, whose blood made Scotland free![1]

---

[1] Archibald Campbell, first Marquis of Argyll, who put the crown on the head of Charles II. in the year 1651, and ten years afterwards was executed by the ungrateful recipient of his loyal devotion.

CLAPHAM

Bright be thy greenery, and sweet thy grass,
    Fair-memoried Clapham ! for there lived in thee,
Far from the selfish strife of class with class,
    A pure white-vested gospel company,
Who brewed rich brewst of Christian love to soothe
    The soreness of the time. The world will still
Paint Nature's face, and bastardise the truth
    With blazoned lies and meretricious skill ;
But, while they fed their gaze with gilded shows,
    Ye ploughed and delved, and sowed the loamy lea
With germing seed that gentle-bladed grows
    Into the branchy firmness of a tree
Dropping rich fruit, from whose rare fulness Fame
Weaves leafy crowns to grace each honoured name.

LALEHAM

(An academy for young ladies at Clapham, under the able superintendence of Miss Pipe.)

BEAUTIFUL Laleham! of most lovely things
   Named with few lovelier, and of things most pure
With purest; angels, might they drop their wings,
   And live as earth-born men on earth, be sure,
Would find meet home and entertainment here,
   With health and innocence, and joy and beauty,
And love and chaste regard, and godly cheer
   To oil the wheels of gently-driving duty.
Oh! if there be who on the barren waste
   Of speculation feed, or through the gray
   Routine of business fret from day to day,
For such there's balm in Laleham, here to taste
   From fresh young lives rare wealth of easy graces,
   Bright eyes, warm hearts, smooth brows, and shining faces.

TAYMOUTH CASTLE

A PIECE of England, ramparted around
   With strength of Highland Ben and heather brae,
   Art thou, fair Taymouth, with thy long array
Of stately trees and stretch of grassy ground,
   Soft with ancestral moss, and thy fair flow
Of the clear amber stream in winding reaches,
That laves the roots of smooth wide-branching beeches,
   With swirl of waters murmuring deep and low.
Who lauds not these is blind; but chiefly I
   Would praise the noble lady of the land,
Who, strong in love and fruitful energy,
   With genial blandness tempers high command,
And holds all hearts with gently-powerful sway,
Like the mild sun that rules the blooming May.

TO HER GRACE THE DUCHESS OF SUTHERLAND

(A reminiscence of 18th September 1881 in Dunrobin Castle.)

FAREWELL, Dunrobin, with thy castled towers,
   And thy majestic sweep of sounding seas,
   And stout old pines which from the unkindly breeze
Shield the bright vermeil of thy gardened flowers!
And farewell thou, lord of this princely home,
   Who not light pleasure made thy fleeting good,
   But with rich life to sow the solitude,
And from the waste redeem the fruitful loam.
But chiefly thou, fair lady, who dost breathe
   Sweet breath of piety through these ducal halls,
   And with rare gospel blossoms dost enwreathe
   The stately splendour of the blazoned walls;
Farewell, and where thou goest, dwell with Thee
God's peace, as thy fair presence dwells with me!

BONSKEID

(The residence of George Freeland Barbour, Esq., near Killiecrankie.)

WHAT scene is here? O come and see and look,
    And feed upon the glory of the land!
Here God speaks forth His will, not in a book,
    The cold gray track of a once living hand,
But in a sea of growth that overflows
    The soul with wonder. Wealth of birchen tresses
Spread with diffusive leafy grace that knows
    No limit to its wandering wildernesses
Of vegetive life. Poor man must count his gains;
    God knows no losses, hath no name for death;
    What we call death is but the march of breath
To other bloods to course in other veins;
    Nature scorns check, and from the pruning-knife
    Rises more bold to more triumphant life.

LOCH BAA

(A beautiful lake in the centre of Mull, where his Grace of Argyll has a shooting lodge, the summer residence of Dr. W. Cumming, Kinellan, Edinburgh.)

FAREWELL, Loch Baa, where oft in thoughtful mood
   Well-pleased I mused in light-wing'd summer hours,
   Drinking in virtue from the breezy powers,
That swept thy soft green slopes, and curled thy flood;
And oft-time clomb thy leafy-skirted braes,
   Cheered by shrill pipings of the plumy clan,
   And from the home of snowy ptarmigan
Surveyed the world of Bens with glad amaze;
   Nor in the white cot failed the genial lord
Who freely poured the brightly-bubbling wine,
   And with rare finny capture spread the board;
Whose praise shall live, my friend of brow benign,
   Whose heart with fretful thought was never stirred,
   Nor his tongue tainted with one loveless word.

ABSENTEE PROPRIETORS

WHO owns these ample hills?—a lord who lives
    Ten months in London, and in Scotland two;
O'er the wide moors, with gun in hand, he drives;
    And, Scotland, this is all he knows of you!
Your tongue, your thoughts, your soul are strange to
    him;
    Your faith, your courage, and your patience true,
Touch him as near as when, with hasty limb,
    He brushes from his boot the mountain dew.
Your sweatful cottar plodding on the hill,
    Your sober church, your priestless sacraments,
He loveth not, who loveth these—to kill
    The guarded game, and swell the squandered rents.
These be thy masters, Scotland!—these the men
Who make thy people vanish from the glen!

BEN MUICDUIBHE

O'ER broad Muicduibhe sweeps the keen cold blast,
    Far whirrs the snow-bred, white-winged ptarmigan,
    Sheer sink the cliffs to dark Loch Etagan,
And all the hill with shattered rock lies waste.
Here brew ship-foundering storms their force divine,
    Here gush the fountains of wild-flooding rivers;
    Here the strong thunder frames the bolt that shivers
The giant strength of the old twisted pine.
Yet, even here, on the bare waterless brow
    Of granite ruin, I found a purple flower,
A delicate flower, as fair as aught, I trow,
    That toys with zephyrs in my lady's bower.
So Nature blends her powers; and he is wise
Who to his strength no gentlest grace denies.

VENICE

City of palaces, Venice, once enthroned
    Secure, a queen mid fence of flashing waters,
Whom East and West with rival homage owned,
    A wealthy mother with fair trooping daughters,
What art thou now? Thy walls are gray and old,
    In thy lone halls the spider weaves his woof,
A leprous crust creeps o'er thy house of gold,
    And the cold rain drips through thy pictured roof.
The frequent ringing of thy churchly bells
    Proclaims a faith but half-believed by few;
Thy palaces are trimmed into hotels,
    And travelling strangers, a vague-wondering crew,
Noting thy stones, with guide-book in their hand,
Leave half the wealth that lingers in the land.

LORD BYRON AND THE ARMENIAN CONVENT

And lived he here? And could this sweet green isle
   Volcanic stuff to his hot heart afford,
That he might nurse his wrath, and vent his bile
   On gods and men, this proud, mistempered lord?
Alas! poor lord, to this soft leafy nest,
   Where only pure and heavenly thoughts should dwell,
He brought, and bore and cherished in his breast,
   A home-bred devil, and a native hell.
Unhappy lord! If this be genius, then
   Grant me, O God, a Muse with sober sweep,
That I may eat and drink with common men,
   Joy with their joys, and with their weeping weep:
Better to chirp mild loves in lowly bower,
Than soar through stormy skies, with hatred for my dower.

III

HISTORICAL BALLADS

ANCRUM MOOR

A HISTORICAL BALLAD

King Henry was a rampant loon,
    No Turk more bold than he
To tread the land with iron shoon
    And tramp with royal glee.

God made him king of England; there
    His royal lust had scope
Tightly to hold beneath his thumb
    People and peer and Pope.

And bishops' craft and lawyers' craft
    Were cobwebs light to him,
And law and right were blown like chaff
    Before his lordly whim.

And many a head of saint and sage
  In ghastly death lay low,
That never a man on English ground
  Might say King Henry no.

Now he would swallow Scotland too
  To glut his kingly maw,
And sent his ships, two hundred sail,
  Bewest North Berwick Law.

And he hath sworn by force to weld
  Two kingdoms into one,
When Scotland's Queen with Scotland's rights,
  Is wed to England's son.

And he hath heaped the quay of Leith
  With devastation dire,
And swept fair Embro's stately town
  Three days with raging fire.

And he hath hired two red-cross loons,[1]
  False Lennox and Glencairn,

---

[1] The Border clans who had been induced to side with Henry wore the red cross of St. George as a badge to distinguish them from the patriotic party. The defection of some prominent members of the Scottish nobility from the national cause on this occasion was not, I am afraid, a solitary instance of baseness, which never bears a fouler front than when found in their class.

From royal Henry's graceless grace
    A traitor's wage to earn.

And he hath said to the warders twain—
    Sir Ralph and stout Sir Bryan—
'Ride north, and closely pare the claws
    Of that rude Scottish lion.

'And all the land benorth Carlisle
    That your good sword secures,
Teviotdale and Lauderdale,
    And the Merse with all its moors,
Land of the Douglas, Ker, and Scott,
    My seal hath made it yours.'

And they have crossed from Carter Fell,
    And laid the fields all bare;
And they have harried Jeddart town,
    And spoiled the abbey there.

And they have ravaged hearth and hall,
    With steel untaught to spare
Or tottering eld, or screaming babe,
    Or tearful lady fair.

And they have come with snorting speed,
    Plashing through mire and mud,
And plunged with hot and haughty hoof
    Through Teviot's silver flood.

And past the stronghold of the Ker[1]
    Like rattling hail they pour,
Right in the face of Penilheugh,
    And up to Ancrum Moor.

'Where be these caitiff Scots?' outcries
    Layton, with hasty fume.
'There!' cries Sir Eure; 'the cowards crouch
    Behind the waving broom.

'Have at them, boys! they may not stand
    Before our strong-hoofed mass;
Like clouds they come, and like the drift
    Of rainless clouds they pass!'

'Not so, Sir Eure! ye do not well
    Thus with light word to scorn

---

[1] Ancrum House, now the residence of Sir William Scott of Ancrum, but at the date of the ballad possessed by a branch of the noble race of the Kers.

The Douglas blood, the strong right arm
    Of Bruce at Bannockburn.

'Lo! where they rise behind the broom
    And stand in bristling pride,
Sharp as the jag of a gray sea-crag
    That flouts the billowy tide.

'With six-foot lances sharply set
    They stand in serried lines,
Like Macedonian phalanx old,
    Or rows of horrid pines.'

Sir Eure was hot: he might not hear,
    Nor pause to weigh the chances,
But spurred his steed in mid career
    Upon the frieze of lances.

Madly they plunge with foaming speed
    On that sharp fence of steel,
And on the ground with bleeding flanks
    They tumble, toss, and reel.

Charge upon charge; but all in vain
    The red-cross troop advances—

Rider and horse, high heaped in death,
    Lay sprawling 'neath the lances.

But what is this that now I see?
    In battailous array
Matrons and maids from Ancrum town
    Are mingled in the fray.

A goodly band; not Sparta bred
    More valiant-hearted maids
Than these that front the fight to-day
    With pitchforks and with spades.

And as they come, 'Broomhouse!' they cry;
    These butcher loons shall rue
Their damnèd force on that fair dame
    Whom at Broomhouse they slew.[1]

And there stands one, and leads the van,—
    A Maxton[2] maid, not tall,

---

[1] In one of their savage raids, the troops of the warder had burnt the tower of Broomhouse, and in it its lady, a noble and aged matron, with her whole family.—TYTLER.

[2] A village on the Tweed, about two miles north of Ancrum Moor, once very populous, and still marked by an old cross.

But with heroic soul supreme
    She soars above them all.

With giant stroke she flails about,
    And heaps a score of dead,
That bring—oh woe! a vengeful troop
    Upon her single head.

With swoop of trenchant blades they come,
    And cut her legs away,
And look that she shall straightway fall
    On ground and bite the clay.

Say, is it by St. Bothan's power,
    Or by St. Boswell's grace,
That still she fights, and swings her arms,
    And stoutly holds her place?

I know not; but true men were there,
    Who saw her stand a while
Fighting, till streams of her brave blood
    Gave riches to the soil;

And then she fell; and true men there,
    Upon the blood-stained moor

Upraised a stone to tell her fame,
    That ever shall endure.

All praise to Humes, and Kers, and Scotts!
    But fair Maid Lilliard's deed
Shall in green honour keep this spot,
    While Teviot runs to Tweed!

MERLIN AND KENTIGERN

A LEGEND OF TWEEDDALE

Come with me fair maiden, Lilias,
    Come and sit a space with me,
Where the Powsail purls and prattles
    Gently by this old thorn tree.[1]

Come and stir good thoughts within me,
    With bright looks of kindly cheer;
Sweetly flows an old man's story
    Where the young are fond to hear.

Yesterday, when I was wandering
    O'er the Broad Law's treeless back,
Came a mist, a white mist floating
    Slowly o'er the moory track.

---

[1] The thorn-tree stands on the burn, about fifteen yards above its junction with the Tweed, below the church of Drummelzier. Here the local tradition has it that the Enchanter was buried.

And ever as it travelled lightly
    Where the fitful breeze might be,
It took new shapes of strangest seeming
    That looked weirdly upon me:

Now a whale, and now an ostrich,
    With a neck of longest span;
Now a camel, now a white bear,
    Now a snowy-locked old man.

And I thought on old man Merlin,
    Merlin, wizard of the Tweed,
Moaning o'er the tway-cleft kingdom,
    Wailing o'er his waning creed.

For he was a heathen, Lilias,
    Mighty man of place and pride,
Counsellor and bard and prophet
    In the kingdom of Strathclyde.

And when Roderick, to the false gods
    False, and faithful to the true,
In the battle of Arderydd [1]
    Slew the mightful Gwenddoleu;

---

[1] Mr. Skene, in an interesting paper in the *Proceedings of the Society of Antiquarians*, February 1865, fixes the site of this battle with great

Merlin old, his bard and prophet,
    Cleaving to the Cymric creed,
Moaning o'er the lost Sun-worship,
    Wandered lonely by the Tweed:

Seeking death, but might not find it;
    For he deemed it sin to die
With a self-implanted dagger
    In the bright Sun's beaming eye.

And he came to where Drummelzier's
    Kirk looks o'er the Powsail brook;
And sadly here, with thoughtful brooding,
    On a stone his seat he took.

Here he sate, with none to friend him
    In his sorrow and his dool,
But his little dog, a black one,
    And a young pig white as wool.[1]

---

probability not far from Longtown, on the great road between that town and Langholm, near the junction of the Liddell and the Esk.

[1] The black dog is a familiar appendage of necromancy and wizardry; but the little pig is peculiarly Welsh, and holds a prominent place in the oldest Cymric poetry. There is a whole class of poems attributed to Merlin, beginning with 'Listen, O little pig! O happy little pig!' which Stephen, in his literature of the Cymri, considers to be symbolical of the Welsh people. How the little snouted creature

Sate and looked, when lo! a figure
    Cloaked and cowled, with solemn gait
Through the shower and through the sun-glint
    Came where wizard Merlin sate:

Came as one that hath a message
    Where delay might father loss,
On his breast a death's-head broidered,
    In his skinny hand a cross.

'Who art thou,' cried Merlin, 'coming
    From the East where dwell my foes?
I have here enough of sorrows,
    Let me feed upon my woes!

'Cause have I to hate the traitor
    Who hath laid my monarch low;
Spare to triumph rudely o'er me,
    Prostrate in my utter woe!

'Cause have I to hate the Christian;
    Hence, and give mine eyes release

---

came to attain this dignity he does not explain; but it is no doubt a relic of the rural economy of the oldest times, when the δῖος ὑφορβός, the 'divine swineherd,' was deemed worthy of occupying a prominent position among the retainers of a Greek kingship.

From thy death's-heads and thy crosses!
　　Let old Merlin die in peace.'

'Fond old man, I may not leave thee;
　　I am here by God's command,
With dear balm of benediction
　　Near thy bed in death to stand.

'I am Kentigern: my mother,
　　Not far from the Isle of May,
Daughter of the king of Lothian,
　　Bore me in a wondrous way.

'Saint Theneu, my blissful mother,
　　Whom the spiteful waves did toss
Rudely, in a fragile shallop
　　Prisoned, bore me at Culross.

'And St. Serf, from where Loch Leven
　　Laves the roots of Lomond Ben,
Washed me throughly in the water
　　Of regeneration then.

'And my mother there devoted
　　Me to God, the One, the True,

To the savage West to wander,
    And convert the heathen crew.

'Bless the Lord this day, old Merlin:
    In the dear name of Theneu,
I am come with God's salvation,
    On the tree who died for you.'

'Mock me not, thou sallow shaveling!
    By yon God that rides on high,
In the pure old Druid worship
    I have lived, and I will die.

'Gods in guise of man we know not,
    Scourged and pierced and crucified;
God we own above all human,
    Baal careering in his pride:

'Baal, whence flows Fire's holy fountain,
    Pulsing with a pulse of might;
Baal, that o'er yon green Trahenna,[1]
    Streams with floods of holy light;

---

[1] One of those green softly sloping mountains which are the glory of Peeblesshire. It rises right opposite Drummelzier on the north bank of the Tweed, right above the mouth of the Biggar water. The name, like not a few others in the district, is manifestly Welsh or Cornish, not Gaelic.

'Baal, whose voice is in the thunder,
    Rolling far from glen to glen;
Baal, whose glance is lightning darted
    From the blue crest of the Ben;

'Baal, whose fiery virtue melteth
    Crusted ice and stony hail
Into rills that leap redundant,
    Spreading sweetness through the vale;

'Him I own within, without me,
    In the great and in the small,
In the near and in the far off,
    In the each and in the all.

'Tempt me not with human Saviours,
    Gods to handle and to feel!
To the bright broad eye of Heaven,
    Life-dispensing Baal, I kneel.

'Preach the cross to savage Saxons;
    Crosses come when they are nigh;
As old Druid wisdom taught me,
    I have lived and I will die!'

Then with holy hand uplifted
  Spake the saintly Kentigern,
And with swelling eye of pity;
  'Old man, thou hast much to learn.

' But the gnarled oak can no man
  Bend like rush or osier wand;
Take my love, and take my blessing,
  With thee to the Spirit-land.

' Allwhere lives a thoughtful Reason,[1]
  In the sky and in the sod;
Mind, and Thought, and shaping Reason,
  This we worship, one true God.

' Sun and moon, and forky levin,
  Floods by sea, and storms by land,
Are but ministers and servants,
  Tools in the Great Master's hand.

' Take my prayer, and take my blessing;
  Though I may not move thy will,
Whom I serve hath gracious magic
  To bring good from harshest ill.

[1] The λόγος of St. John, and νοῦς of Anaxagoras.

'In His house are many mansions;
　　If thy heart is pure and true,
He can save with stretch of mercy,
　　Merlin old and Gwenddoleu.'

Spake: and with his cloak wrapt round him,
　　Eastward o'er the moor he strode,
Leaving wise old Merlin brooding
　　Strangely o'er the Christian's God.

But his brooding must be barren:
　　Who can change an old man's creed?
Romish Gods might not be devils,
　　But Baal was God for Merlin's need.

With an eye of moody-wandering
　　Gaze, he followed Kentigern,
Where he brushed the purple heather,
　　Where he swept the plumy fern.

And he wandered o'er the moorland,
　　Wrapt in sorrow and in dool,
With his small black dog behind him,
　　And his young pig white as wool;

Wandered till he found a hollow
    Cavern by the river's brim,
Where a witch, a wily lady,
    With a strong spell prisoned him.[1]

And she kept him there, the fell one,
    Till his eyes with age grew dim;
Then the wily fair, the false one,
    Mixed the cup of death for him.

And wayfaring people found him
    Stretched beside the river's brim;
And beneath this ragged thorn-tree,
    Here they dug a grave for him.

And his small black dog they buried,
    And his little pig with him;
And they wailed before the Sun-god
    Sadly by the river's brim.

Weep for him, and kiss me, Lilias,
    Kindly kisses help our need,
When a tearful story moves us
    On the flowery banks of Tweed!

---

[1] *Morte Arthur*, vol. i. ch. 60, Wright's edition.

PEDEN THE PROPHET

(*Scene*—A farmhouse in the parish of Auchinleck, Ayrshire; Peden on his deathbed.)

O MY heart is weary, weary,
    Weary of these times of killing
On the bleeding heart of Scotland,
    All the wrath of man fulfilling!

O my heart is weary, weary
    Of these cruel killing times,
When to serve our Saviour freely
    Is the worst of human crimes!

O my heart is weary, weary
    Of this red rule of the sword!
Earth is grown a hell to Peden;
    Take me to Thy home, dear Lord!

O my heart is weary, weary
    Of God's earth made home for devils,

Justice blind, and Mercy smothered,
　　Judges drunk[1] with bloody revels!

I have lived to see great folly,
　　Faults and folly all our own,
When we placed the crown of Albyn
　　On that wanton boy at Scone!

Fools were we to trust the Stuart,
　　Fools to take the wounded snake
To our breast from where it lay
　　Harmless, bleeding in the brake.

All that Stuart brood were tainted
　　With French poison in the blood,
Basely born of Popish Mary,
　　And a brainless lordling lewd!

Most unwisely wise was Argyll,
　　On his head the crown to lay,
Who should lay the head that crowned him
　　Ingrate!—bleeding on the clay.

---

[1] The Scottish Parliament of 1661 that lent themselves to Charles II. as instruments to crush the very people who had put the crown on his head was called 'The Drunken Parliament.'—*See* DODDS.

O, my country! false men honoured,
  True men trampled in the mud;
Scottish lords in servile council
  Reeling from the vote of blood!

These vext eyes have seen it—manhood
  Banished from the hearts of men,
And God's faithful remnant chased
  With fiendish rage from den to den.

I have seen the Sharp, the Judas,
  Hireling priest of fools and knaves,
Stamping noblest men for felons,
  Shipping God's dear saints for slaves.

I have seen poor innocent children
  Where that Judas swayed the mace,
Golden blue-eyed darlings branded
  With hot iron in the face.

I have seen Dalziel, the savage,
  Surly-mouthed, white-bearded Turk,
Crimsoning the green of Pentland
  With unhallowed butcher work.

I have seen M'Kail, the bright boy,
    With a glory in his face,
When his limbs were crushed and shattered,
    Where that Judas swayed the mace.

I have seen the brazen-fronted,
    Clumsy, coarse-grained Lauderdale,
With his titled harlot bringing
    Kilted thieves to gather mail

From the good and gracious people,
    Who, untrained in courtly ways,
Pour the fervid psalm full-breasted
    From the unbribed heather braes.

I have seen when holy Cargill,
    He and other saintly four,
At the West Port of Dun Edin
    Showed their faces daubed in gore.

Showed their limbs all hacked and hagged
    By a hireling hangman loon,
To make sport to foul-mouthed jesters,
    In the face of sun and moon.

I have seen, when 'neath Cairntable's
    Shadow on a bright May morn,
Came that bloody, swearing Clavers,
    To the Devil's service sworn.

And before the neat white cottage,
    Where the godly carrier dwelt,
In a plunge of fiendish passion,
    Drew the pistol from his belt,

And in face of weeping mother,
    And of screaming children, there
Laid him, with a coarse blaspheming
    Jest, upon a bloody lair.

O my heart is weary, weary
    Of these cruel times of killing,
On the bleeding heart of Scotland,
    All the Devil's spite fulfilling!

O that I might be with Ritchie,
    Where he sleeps in Aird's Moss,
Where the savage, swearing troopers
    Cut him down to Scotland's loss!

O that I might be with Ritchie,
    'Neath the sod with my brave brother,
I, who homeless lived, from one
    Bloody land tossed to another!

O that I might be with Ritchie!
But——

    (*Knocking heard at the door.*)

Who's there?

    [*Enter* Renwick.]

        My son, my son!
    (*Embraces him.*)

Whence and whither?

RENWICK.

        I am wandering
    Houseless through a scattered clan,
To proclaim to ears that love it,
    God's free word of grace to man.

Peden.

Bless thee, brave boy! I am going
    Gently, gladly to my rest,
Where the wicked cease from troubling,
    Where the weary are at rest.

Renwick.

Not so, father,—though 'twere better
    There for me with thee to dwell,
That without thee here in Scotland,
    Which this James hath turned to hell!

Peden.

List to me, my boy, my Renwick,
    In the hour of darkest night
Faithful eyes with prophet vision
    Read the streaks of coming light.

I am dying; but full surely
    God's great truth dies not with me,
That small seed which thanks thy watering,
    Soon shall grow a mighty tree.

God hath shown me in a vision;
    Even now I see the day
When that ass which plays the lion,
    As pure ass revealed shall bray

To the moon. His time is short,
    Of fifty years there lack but two,
To make full the lease of carnage
    To the tiger-hearted crew.

Mark me well! I saw in vision
    Pope and king and cowlèd monk
Doomed to feast upon the vomit
    Of the blood that they had drunk.

Short two years he hath for fooling;
    Thou shalt see it, mark me well,
Cross, and beads, and hempen girdle,
    All the bravery of hell,

On the banks of Thames paraded;
    Thou shalt see the cursèd thing,
Juggled wine and juggled wafers,
    In the palace of the king.

In the palace, in the Savoy,
    In St. John's at Clerkenwell,
Subtle Jesuits are training
    Simple English youths for hell!

What is this? O shame! O sorrow!
    Thou shalt see it, mark me well;
England's king kneels to the Vicar
    Of the Majesty of Hell!

In the temple prankt with idols,
    'Neath the gaudy-pictured dome,
He hath vowed a damned allegiance
    To the scarlet-vested Rome!

Lo! another and another
    Stride he makes that scorns all bounds;
Like a drunken giant blindly
    Striking where the stroke redounds.

To the peaceful halls of learning,
    With no soul beyond the brute,
He doth come, and grimly solemn
    Planteth there his tyrant foot.

O

He hath cast out all the scholars,
   Tramped their Greek books in the mud ;
Who would swear at no king's bidding,
   That bread is flesh and wine is blood.

On the mitred pomp of bishops
   He doth tramp with foot profane—
Some good things are found in bishops—
   But he bribes their faith in vain.

In Lud's town I see the bonfires
   Blazing high, now here now there,
With loud cries of acclamation
   Ringing through the gladsome air.

Ringing doom to James and Popery!
   Soon, right soon, the tide will turn ;
Any little child learns wisdom,
   When his fingers he may burn,

But not James. Supremely seated
   On a throne of vain conceit ;
All the subject world he visions
   Crouching at a despot's feet.

But his dream grows pale and paler,
    Danger bristles round and round ;
All the manly soul of England
    To God's gospel faithful found,

Blares revolt—the child, the daughter
    Flees the father ; son and mother,
Lo ! I see them down the river,
    Through strong storm and rainy pother,

Franceward borne ; and soon the father
    Follows where the narrowed sea
Parts the land of gilded bondage
    From the proud home of the free.

There to plot and fret and dream,
    Ever wilful, never wise ;
Thence once more to challenge fortune,
    For a crown which Right denies.

Rome hath many slaves in Erin's
    Backmost bound ; this gives him hope
With a band of loose marauders
    To make muster for the Pope.

Vainly. On a milk-white charger,
  With a white plume on his head,
From the land of dykes and ditches,
  With redemption in his tread

Comes God's elect warrior, grandly
  Girt about with power divine,
For well-weighed and thoughtful doing.
  Lo! I see on banks of Boyne,

Troops well marshalled in the summer
  Morning's bright and beaming eye,
With green branches in their helmets,
  Marching on to victory!

On they come, right through the current,
  Dash and splash with gallant ease;
While the Pope's crude minions flee,
  Like wicked wasps before the breeze!

Glory, glory! through the midnight
  Strays the gleam of Fate to me;
On thine eyes shall break the dawning
  Of the day that makes us free.

But the brightness of the noonday
    God's high will denies to thee;
Only from the top of Nebo
    Thou the coming grace shalt see.

Fare-thee-well, my joy, my Renwick!
    Thou hast kept thy garments pure;
Thou hast scorned the bribes of traitors,
    What thou doest shall endure.

I go hence. More blest than Peden,
    Stretched to die on nameless bed,
Thou shalt shine, a star with martyrs,
    Who for God's free gospel bled.[1]

---

[1] The noble young preacher, James Renwick, was hanged in the Grassmarket in the month of February 1688, at the early age of twenty-six, for no other crime than the courageous assertion of those principles of constitutional right proclaimed publicly three months later in London by the glorious resolution of 1688.

NOTES

ANCRUM MOOR, p. 167.

The sojourner on the classic banks of the Tweed who may have some floating memories of the confused doings in Scotland about the middle of the sixteenth century, when the tragic history of the unfortunate Queen Mary was being foreshadowed by the state of Scotland at her birth, will probably have the curiosity to visit the ridge of Ancrum Moor, a few miles from St. Boswells, on the Jedburgh Road, a little to the north of the river Teviot, which rolls here through the beautiful domain of the Marquess of Lothian, towards its junction with the Tweed at Kelso. The high ground is well marked to the eye by a row of pine-trees running from west to east, about half a mile long: along this breezy ridge a well-trodden path leads, marking the march of many a patriotic pilgrim on a summer's holiday; and at the east end of the path the pedestrian comes suddenly on a plain stone enclosure, made of the red sandstone of the district, and within the enclosure an erect slab or memorial stone, bearing an inscription easily read as follows:—

> 'Fair Maiden Lilliard lies beneath this stane;
> Small was her stature, but mickle was her fame;
> Upon the English loons she laid full many thumps,
> And when her legs were cuttit off she fought upon her stumps.'

The affair in which this Border Amazon played such a stout part, took place in the year 1544, and was one of the bloody sequels of the insolent course of dictation to Scotland which Henry VIII. commenced immediately after the decease of James V., the father of Queen Mary. This imperious Tudor, accustomed, with the help of the strong-willed Machiavelian Cromwell, to bear down everything before him at home, and looking eagerly about him for some field in which he might find compensation to England for her reluctantly abandoned dream of a French inheritance, found nothing to his imagination more plausible than the offer of the hand of his young son Edward to the infant queen of Scotland; and this project he could the more hopefully cherish, as he happened at that time to hold a large number of notable Scottish prisoners in his keep from the recent battle of Solway Moss. The union of the kingdoms, which this project might have secured more than a century and a half before it actually took place, was a matter which many of the most far-sighted and best-disposed statesmen in Scotland were not unwilling to entertain, especially as at that moment an alliance with Henry, the prominent champion of Protestantism, might serve to secure the nation against the machinations of the still powerful Catholic party in the country. But the insolent manner in which the self-willed despot made his matrimonial proposals effectually prevented their acceptance: his demands, in which he assumed the tone of Edward Longshanks, roused the pride of the people, whom he ought rather to have conciliated; and the consequence was, that after a series of hasty plunges into war to enforce his unreasonable claims, he made foes of his best friends, and ultimately threw the nation back into its old French alliance, and a French matrimonial connection to boot. In the year 1544, two rapacious assaults were made by this bloody suitor on the country of his son's spear-purchased bride: the one by sea upon Edinburgh, under the conduct of the Earl of Hertford; the other on the Border counties, led by Sir Ralph Eure and Sir Bryan Layton. It is this invasion which, after ravaging the country as far as Melrose, with a series of horrors only too common in those days, ended in the repulse of the invaders and the death of the two wardens at the battle of Ancrum Moor.

In the ballad, I have followed closely the historical account as given by Tytler in his *History of Scotland*, except that I have omitted the previous affair at Melrose altogether, and brought the invaders directly down upon Ancrum. Any minute details of strategical movements — if the military movements of those times might merit the name—previous to the victorious result, would have been not less foreign to the genius of the Border ballad than destitute of all historical value.

I ought to add, that the tradition of the heroine of the fray continuing the fight on her stumps after her legs were cut off, and which no doubt has its humorous aspect, is founded on the acknowledged historical fact that a body of women did join in the battle: as little can there be any doubt that the stout little maid of Maxton was the first in the fray, and distinguished herself in a fashion that naturally led to the humorous exaggeration contained in the memorial verses. Such exaggerations belong to the very essence of the popular ballad, and must be taken kindly, like not a few things in Homer that mar the sublime in some of his most effective passages.

MERLIN AND KENTIGERN, p. 175.

This ballad is founded on a passage in Fordun's *Scotichronicon* (iii. 31), in which Kentigern, or St. Mungo, the patron saint of Glasgow, is brought into communication with Merlin, the well-known Welsh enchanter of the medieval romances. Of course no man accepts Fordun as a voucher for any historical fact; but there is evidence enough, independent of Fordun, to prove that St. Kentigern and Merlin were contemporaries, both being representative characters of a great religious movement in the sixth century—the one representing the advancing cause of Christianity in the Celtic or Cymro-Celtic kingdom of Strathclyde, the other the waning cause of Druidism. The battle of Arderydd, A.D. 573, fought between the Christianised King Rhydderch Hael and the heathen monarch Gwenddoleu, divided the Britons of the west, in point of religion, into two unequal halves, of which the lesser was destined speedily to be absorbed into the larger. Of this threatened absorption, Merlin, the Court bard of Gwenddoleu, in the popular tradition appears as the rueful prophet; there is no hope for him or his sun-worship any more, and he must mope about the hills of the south Highlands, then the central part of the kingdom of Strathclyde, till he dies. This is the historical kernel of the miraculous legends which afterwards grew up on both sides of the struggle round the person of their prominent representatives—legends amply sufficient to prove the social importance of the personages concerned, however transparently fictitious, and often ludicrously childish in their details. Discount the silly miracles so bountifully showered on the saint, and the tricks of devilry so lavishly attributed to the Court minstrel of the heathen king, and you have the lasting truth of popular poetical tradition, which Aristotle pronounced to be more philosophical than history. The handling which Roger Bacon, and Doctor Faust, and other such victims of popular prejudice received in the middle ages, may teach us that we are only performing an act of historical justice when we represent Merlin, the Welsh enchanter, in a much more noble light than that in which he appears in the medieval romances, in the pages of the monkish chronicles, or even in the classical portraiture of Lord Tennyson. The facts alluded to in the verses, so far as Kentigern is concerned, will be found in the late Bishop Forbes's *Kalendar of Scottish Saints* (Edinburgh, 1872); in Skene's *Celtic Scotland*, ii. 179; and in *The Legends of St. Kentigern, his Friends and Disciples*, by the late Professor Stevenson (Edinburgh, 1872); and in regard to Merlin, in *Stephen's Literature of the Cymri* (London, 1876); in the *Morte Arthur;* in Professor Veitch's interesting and instructive volume on *The History and Poetry of the Scottish Border* (Glasgow, 1878); and in the recent work of Mr. Beveridge on *Culross and Tulliallan* (Edinburgh, Blackwood, 1885).

PEDEN THE PROPHET, p. 185.

The heroic struggle for liberty of conscience carried on for fifty years by the Scottish Covenanters against the insolent despotism of the Stuarts, and the servile sycophancy, and ceremonial pedantry of the Anglican bishops, has never received to its just extent that grateful recognition which it deserves from the literary mind of the country. The reason of this lies partly in the tendency so natural to a large country like England, to ignore the heroic history of a smaller country with which it has become politically united, partly in the circumstance that even in Presbyterian Scotland not a few of the most influential persons in the upper classes and so-called fashionable world are either Episcopalians by conviction, or given to a certain dainty flirtation with Episcopacy, which Charles II. said was the only religion for a gentleman ; and in either case more apt to look on those noble champions of our Scottish nationality with a narrow sectarian prejudice, than with a large human sympathy. Nevertheless, the truth remains that to these men as much as to any of the noblest names in British constitutional history, we owe the firm foundations of our religious liberties, laid by their foresight and cemented with their blood ; and among these, if not in every respect the greatest, certainly the most picturesque personality, is Alexander Peden, a native of Sorn, in Ayrshire, commonly called Peden the Prophet. The fact that he lived, through an adventurous and sorely-tried manhood, to nearly the end of these 'killing times,' constitutes him on the poetic stage a fit person to rehearse in memory the principal events of that lawless period, from the famous protesting stool of Jenny Geddes in 1637 to the Bloody Assizes of the atrocious Judge Jefferies in the autumn of 1685 ; while his traditional character as a prophet marks him out no less aptly as the forecaster of the last years of that sad series of persistent blunders which led to the battle of the Boyne and the final ejection of James II. from a position which he claimed to occupy, not for the public good, of which he was the legal guardian, but for the gratification of his own blind will, and the pampering of his inordinate conceit. I have therefore represented him as on his deathbed reviewing the atrocities of the Stuart regimen up to January 1686, the date of his death ; and used the historical fact of the visit of the youthful preacher *Renwick* to the dying prophet as a fit occasion for putting into his mouth a few significant utterances with regard to the immediate future. The general outline of the events of those fifty years of noble struggle may be assumed as sufficiently known to the readers of Macaulay's pictorial pages; the more detailed facts which the ballad presents in rhythmical form will be found in the admirable work by James Dodds, *The Fifty Years Struggle of the Covenanters* (Edinburgh, Douglas, 1860); and in the no less interesting volumes, *The Martyr Graves of Scotland*, by the Rev. J. H. Thomson (Edinburgh, Johnstone, Hunter, & Co., 1875), and *The Homes, Haunts, and Battlefields of the Covenanters*, by A. B. Todd (Edinburgh, Gemmell, 1866).

THE END

Printed by R. & R. CLARK, *Edinburgh.*

www.ingramcontent.com/pod-product-compliance
Lightning Source LLC
Chambersburg PA
CBHW031818220426
43662CB00007B/701